Veloce *Classic Reprint* Series

Toyota
Celica GT-Four

Those Were The Days ... Series
Alpine Trials & Rallies 1910-1973 (Pfundner)
American 'Independent' Automakers – AMC to Willys 1945 to 1960 (Mort)
American Station Wagons – The Golden Era 1950-1975 (Mort)
American Trucks of the 1950s (Mort)
American Trucks of the 1960s (Mort)
American Woodies 1928-1953 (Mort)
Anglo-American Cars from the 1930s to the 1970s (Mort)
Austerity Motoring (Bobbitt)
Austins, The last real (Peck)
Brighton National Speed Trials (Gardiner)
British and European Trucks of the 1970s (Peck)
British Drag Racing – The early years (Pettitt)
British Lorries of the 1950s (Bobbitt)
British Lorries of the 1960s (Bobbitt)
British Touring Car Racing (Collins)
British Police Cars (Walker)
British Woodies (Peck)
Café Racer Phenomenon, The (Walker)
Don Hayter's MGB Story – The birth of the MGB in MG's Abingdon Design & Development Office (Hayter)
Drag Bike Racing in Britain – From the mid '60s to the mid '80s (Lee)
Dune Buggy Phenomenon, The (Hale)
Dune Buggy Phenomenon Volume 2, The (Hale)
Endurance Racing at Silverstone in the 1970s & 1980s (Parker)
Hot Rod & Stock Car Racing in Britain in the 1980s (Neil)
Mercedes-Benz Trucks (Peck)
MG's Abingdon Factory (Moylan)
Motor Racing at Brands Hatch in the Seventies (Parker)
Motor Racing at Brands Hatch in the Eighties (Parker)
Motor Racing at Crystal Palace (Collins)
Motor Racing at Goodwood in the Sixties (Gardiner)
Motor Racing at Nassau in the 1950s & 1960s (O'Neil)
Motor Racing at Oulton Park in the 1960s (McFadyen)
Motor Racing at Oulton Park in the 1970s (McFadyen)
Motor Racing at Thruxton in the 1970s (Grant-Braham)
Motor Racing at Thruxton in the 1980s (Grant-Braham)
Superprix – The Story of Birmingham Motor Race (Page & Collins)
Three Wheelers (Bobbitt)

Great Cars
Austin-Healey – A celebration of the fabulous 'Big' Healey (Piggott)
Jaguar E-type (Thorley)
Jaguar Mark 1 & 2 (Thorley)
Triumph TR – TR2 to 6: The last of the traditional sports cars (Piggott)

Rally Giants Series
Audi Quattro (Robson)
Austin Healey 100-6 & 3000 (Robson)
Fiat 131 Abarth (Robson)
Ford Escort MkI (Robson)
Ford Escort RS Cosworth & World Rally Car (Robson)
Ford Escort RS1800 (Robson)
Lancia Delta 4WD/Integrale (Robson)
Lancia Stratos (Robson)
Mini Cooper/Mini Cooper S (Robson)
Peugeot 205 T16 (Robson)
Saab 96 & V4 (Robson)
Subaru Impreza (Robson)
Toyota Celica GT4 (Robson)

WSC Giants
Audi R8 (Wagstaff)
Ferrari 312P & 312PB (Collins & McDonough)
Gulf-Mirage 1967 to 1982 (McDonough)
Matra Sports Cars – MS620, 630, 650, 660 & 670 – 1966 to 1974 (McDonough)

Biographies
A Chequered Life – Graham Warner and the Chequered Flag (Hesletine)
A Life Awheel – The 'auto' biography of W de Forte (Skelton)
Amédée Gordini ... a true racing legend (Smith)
André Lefebvre, and the cars he created at Voisin and Citroën (Beck)
Chris Carter at Large – Stories from a lifetime in motorcycle racing (Carter & Skelton)
Cliff Allison, The Official Biography of – From the Fells to Ferrari (Gauld)
Edward Turner – The Man Behind the Motorcycles (Clew)
Driven by Desire – The Desiré Wilson Story
First Principles – The Official Biography of Keith Duckworth (Burr)
Inspired to Design – F1 cars, Indycars & racing tyres: the autobiography of Nigel Bennett (Bennett)
Jack Sears, The Official Biography of – Gentleman Jack (Gauld)
Jim Redman – 6 Times World Motorcycle Champion: The Autobiography (Redman)
John Chatham – 'Mr Big Healey' – The Official Biography (Burr)
The Lee Noble Story (Wilkins)
Mason's Motoring Mayhem – Tony Mason's hectic life in motorsport and television (Mason)
Raymond Mays' Magnificent Obsession (Apps)
Pat Moss Carlsson Story, The – Harnessing Horsepower (Turner)
'Sox' – Gary Hocking – the forgotten World Motorcycle Champion (Hughes)
Tony Robinson – The biography of a race mechanic (Wagstaff)
Virgil Exner – Visioneer: The Official Biography of Virgil M Exner Designer Extraordinaire (Grist)

General
1½-litre GP Racing 1961-1965 (Whitelock)
AC Two-litre Saloons & Buckland Sportscars (Archibald)
Alpine & Renault – The Development of the Revolutionary Turbo F1 Car 1968 to 1979 (Smith)
Alpine & Renault – The Sports Prototypes 1963 to 1969 (Smith)
Alpine & Renault – The Sports Prototypes 1973 to 1978 (Smith)
An Austin Anthology (Stringer)
An Incredible Journey (Falls & Reisch)
Anatomy of the Classic Mini (Huthert & Ely)
Anatomy of the Works Minis (Moylan)
Austin Cars 1948 to 1990 – a pictorial history (Rowe)
Autodrome (Collins & Ireland)
Automotive A-Z, Lane's Dictionary of Automotive Terms (Lane)
Automotive Mascots (Kay & Springate)
Bahamas Speed Weeks, The (O'Neil)
Bluebird CN7 (Stevens)
BMC Competitions Department Secrets (Turner, Chambers & Browning)
British at Indianapolis, The (Wagstaff)
British Café Racers (Cloesen)
British Cars, The Complete Catalogue of, 1895-1975 (Culshaw & Horrobin)
British Custom Motorcycles – The Brit Chop – choppers, cruisers, bobbers & trikes (Cloesen)
BRM – A Mechanic's Tale (Salmon)
BRM V16 (Ludvigsen)
BSA Bantam Bible, The (Henshaw)
BSA Motorcycles – the final evolution (Jones)
Carrera Panamericana, La (Tipler)
Car-tastrophes – 80 automotive atrocities from the past 20 years (Honest John, Fowler)
Chrysler 300 – America's Most Powerful Car 2nd Edition (Ackerson)
Chrysler PT Cruiser (Ackerson)
Citroën DS (Bobbitt)
Classic British Car Electrical Systems (Astley)
Cobra – The Real Thing! (Legate)
Competition Car Aerodynamics 3rd Edition (McBeath)
Competition Car Composites A Practical Handbook (Revised 2nd Edition) (McBeath)
Concept Cars, How to illustrate and design – New 2nd Edition (Dewey)
Cortina – Ford's Bestseller (Robson)
Cosworth – The Search for Power (6th edition) (Robson)
Coventry Climax Racing Engines (Hammill)
Daily Mirror 1970 World Cup Rally 40, The (Robson)
Drive on the Wild Side, A – 20 Extreme Driving Adventures From Around the World (Weaver)
East German Motor Vehicles in Pictures (Suhr/Weinreich)
Essential Guide to Driving in Europe, The (Parish)
Fast Ladies – Female Racing Drivers 1888 to 1970 (Bouzanquet)
Fate of the Sleeping Beauties, The (op de Weegh/Hottendorff/op de Weegh)
Ferrari 288 GTO, The Book of the (Sackey)
Ferrari 333 SP (O'Neil)
Fiat & Abarth 124 Spider & Coupé (Tipler)
Fiat & Abarth 500 & 600 – 2nd Edition (Bobbitt)
Fiats, Great Small (Ward)
Ford Cleveland 335-Series V8 engine 1970 to 1982 – The Essential Source Book (Hammill)
Ford F100/F150 Pick-up 1948-1996 (Ackerson)
Ford F150 Pick-up 1997-2005 (Ackerson)
Ford Focus WRC (Robson)
Ford GT – Then, and Now (Streather)
Ford GT40 (Legate)
Ford Midsize Muscle – Fairlane, Torino & Ranchero (Cranswick)
Ford Model Y (Roberts)
Ford Small Block V8 Racing Engines 1962-1970 – The Essential Source Book (Hammill)
Formula One – The Real Score? (Harvey)
Formula 5000 Motor Racing, Back then ... and back now (Lawson)
Forza Minardi! (Vigar)
The Good, the Mad and the Ugly ... not to mention Jeremy Clarkson (Dron)
Grand Prix Ferrari – The Years of Enzo Ferrari's Power, 1948-1980 (Pritchard)
Grand Prix Ford – DFV-powered Formula 1 Cars (Robson)
GT – The World's Best GT Cars 1953-73 (Dawson)
Hillclimbing & Sprinting – The Essential Manual (Short & Wilkinson)
Honda NSX (Long)
Immortal Austin Seven (Morgan)
Karmann-Ghia Coupé & Convertible (Bobbitt)
Kawasaki Triples Bible, The (Walker)
Kris Meeke – Intercontinental Rally Challenge Champion (McBride)
Lancia 037 (Collins)
Lancia Delta HF Integrale (Blaettel & Wagner)
Lancia Delta Integrale (Collins)
Le Mans Panoramic (Ireland)
Lexus Story, The (Long)
Maserati 250F In Focus (Pritchard)
Maximum Mini (Booij)
Mercedes G-Wagen (Long)
MG, Made in Abingdon (Frampton)
MGA (Price Williams)
MGB & MGB GT– Expert Guide (Auto-doc Series) (Williams)
MGB Electrical Systems Updated & Revised Edition (Astley)
Micro Trucks (Mort)
Microcars at Large! (Quellin)
Mini Cooper – The Real Thing! (Tipler)
Mini Minor to Asia Minor (West)
Mitsubishi Lancer Evo, The Road Car & WRC Story (Long)
Montlhéry, The Story of the Paris Autodrome (Boddy)
MOPAR Muscle – Barracuda, Dart & Valiant 1960-1980 (Cranswick)
Morgan Maverick (Lawrence)
Morgan 3 Wheeler – back to the future!, The (Dron)
Morris Minor, 70 Years on the Road (Newell)
Motor Racing – Reflections of a Lost Era (Carter)
Motor Racing – The Pursuit of Victory 1930-1962 (Carter)
Motor Racing – The Pursuit of Victory 1963-1972 (Wyatt/Sears)
Motor Racing Heroes – The Stories of 100 Greats (Newman)
Motorcycle Apprentice (Cakebread)
Motorcycle GP Racing in the 1960s (Pereira)
Motorcycle Racing with the Continental Circus 1920-1970 (Pereira)
Motorcycle Road & Racing Chassis Designs (Noakes)
Motorcycling in the '50s (Clew)
Motorhomes, The Illustrated History (Jenkinson)
Motorsport In colour, 1950s (Wainwright)
MV Agusta Fours, The book of the classic (Falloon)
N.A.R.T. – A concise history of the North American Racing Team 1957 to 1983 (O'Neil)
Nissan 300ZX & 350Z – The Z-Car Story (Long)
Nissan GT-R Supercar: Born to race (Gorodji)
Northeast American Sports Car Races 1950-1959 (O'Neil)
Norton Commando Bible – All models 1968 to 1978 (Henshaw)
Nothing Runs – Misadventures in the Classic, Collectable & Exotic Car Biz (Slutsky)
Off-Road Giants! (Volume 1) – Heroes of 1960s Motorcycle Sport (Westlake)
Off-Road Giants! (Volume 2) – Heroes of 1960s Motorcycle Sport (Westlake)
Off-Road Giants! (Volume 3) – Heroes of 1960s Motorcycle Sport (Westlake)
Pass the Theory and Practical Driving Tests (Gibson & Hoole)
Peking to Paris 2007 (Young)
Pontiac Firebird – New 3rd Edition (Cranswick)
Preston Tucker & Others (Linde)
RAC Rally Action! (Gardiner)
Racing Colours – Motor Racing Compositions 1908-2009 (Newman)
Racing Line – British motorcycle racing in the golden age of the big single (Guntrip)
Rallye Sport Fords: The Inside Story (Moreton)
The Red Baron's Ultimate Ducati Desmo Manual (Cabrera Choclán)
Renewable Energy Home Handbook, The (Porter)
Roads with a View – England's greatest views and how to find them by road (Corfield)
Rolls-Royce Silver Shadow/Bentley T Series Corniche & Camargue – Revised & Enlarged Edition (Bobbitt)
Rolls-Royce Silver Spirit, Silver Spur & Bentley Mulsanne 2nd Edition (Bobbitt)
Rootes Cars of the 50s, 60s & 70s – Hillman, Humber, Singer, Sunbeam & Talbot (Rowe)
Rover P4 (Bobbitt)
Runways & Racers (O'Neil)
Russian Motor Vehicles – Soviet Limousines 1930-2003 (Kelly)
Russian Motor Vehicles – The Czarist Period 1784 to 1917 (Kelly)
RX-7 – Mazda's Rotary Engine Sportscar (Updated & Revised New Edition) (Long)
Scooters & Microcars, The A-Z of Popular (Dan)
Scooter Lifestyle (Grainger)
Scooter Mania! – Recollections of the Isle of Man International Scooter Rally (Jackson)
Singer Story: Cars, Commercial Vehicles, Bicycles & Motorcycle (Atkinson)
Sleeping Beauties USA – abandoned classic cars & trucks (Marek)
SM – Citroën's Maserati-engined Supercar (Long & Claverol)
Speedway – Auto racing's ghost tracks (Collins & Ireland)
Sprite Caravans, The Story of (Jenkinson)
Standard Motor Company, The Book of the (Robson)
Steve Hole's Kit Car Cornucopia – Cars, Companies, Stories, Facts & Figures: the UK's kit car scene since 1949 (Hole)
Subaru Impreza: The Road Car And WRC Story (Long)
Supercar, How to Build your own (Thompson)
Tales from the Toolbox (Oliver)
Tatra – The Legacy of Hans Ledwinka, Updated & Enlarged Collector's Edition of 1500 copies (Margolius & Henry)
Taxi! The Story of the 'London' Taxicab (Bobbitt)
This Day in Automotive History (Corey)
To Boldly Go – twenty six vehicle designs that dared to be different (Hull)
Toleman Story, The (Hilton)
Toyota Celica & Supra, The Book of Toyota's Sports Coupés (Long)
Toyota MR2 Coupés & Spyders (Long)
Triumph & Standard Cars 1945 to 1984 (Warrington)
Triumph Bonneville Bible (59-83) (Henshaw)
Triumph Bonneville!, Save the – The inside story of the Meriden Workers' Co-op (Rosamond)
Triumph Motorcycles & the Meriden Factory (Hancox)
Triumph Speed Twin & Thunderbird Bible (Woolridge)
Triumph Tiger Cub Bible (Estall)
Triumph Trophy Bible (Woolridge)
Triumph TR6 (Kimberley)
TT Talking – The TT's most exciting era – As seen by Manx Radio TT's lead commentator 2004-2012 (Lambert)
Two Summers – The Mercedes-Benz W196R Racing Car (Ackerson)
TWR Story, The – Group A (Hughes & Scott)
Unraced (Collins)
Velocette Motorcycles – MSS to Thruxton – Third Edition (Burris)
Vespa – The Story of a Cult Classic in Pictures (Uhlig)
Vincent Motorcycles: The Untold Story since 1946 (Guyony & Parker)
Volkswagen Bus Book, The (Bobbitt)
Volkswagen Bus or Van to Camper, How to Convert (Porter)
Volkswagens of the World (Glen)
VW Beetle Cabriolet – The full story of the convertible Beetle (Bobbitt)
VW Beetle – The Car of the 20th Century (Copping)
VW Bus – 40 Years of Splitties, Bays & Wedges (Copping)
VW Bus Book, The (Bobbitt)
VW Golf: Five Generations of Fun (Copping & Cservenka)
VW – The Air-cooled Era (Copping)
VW T5 Camper Conversion Manual (Porter)
VW Campers (Copping)
Volkswagen Type 3, The book of the – Concept, Design, International Production Models & Development (Glen)
Volvo Estate, The (Hollebone)
You & Your Jaguar XK8/XKR – Buying, Enjoying, Maintaining, Modifying – New Edition (Thorley)
Which Oil? – Choosing the right oils & greases for your antique, vintage, veteran, classic or collector car (Michell)
Wolseley Cars 1948 to 1975 (Rowe)
Works Minis, The Last (Purves & Brenchley)
Works Rally Mechanic (Moylan)

www.veloce.co.uk

Also available ... Apps Download now from www.digital.veloce.co.uk

Hubble & Hattie

Belvedere

Also available ... eBook Download now from www.digital.veloce.co.uk

First published under ISBN: 978-1-84584-184-3 in August 2009 by Veloce Publishing Limited, Veloce House, Parkway Farm Business Park, Middle Farm Way, Poundbury, Dorchester DT1 3AR, England. Fax 01305 268864/Tel 01305 260068/e-mail info@veloce.co.uk/web www.veloce.co.uk or www.velocebooks.com.
Veloce Classic Reprint edition published April 2018
ISBN: 978-1-787113-31-2. UPC: 6-36847-01331-8
© Graham Robson and Veloce Publishing 2009 & 2018. All rights reserved. With the exception of quoting brief passages for the purpose of review, no part of this publication may be recorded, reproduced or transmitted by any means, including photocopying, without the written permission of Veloce Publishing Ltd. Throughout this book logos, model names and designations, etc, have been used for the purposes of identification, illustration and decoration. Such names are the property of the trademark holder as this is not an official publication.
Readers with ideas for automotive books, or books on other transport or related hobby subjects, are invited to write to the editorial director of Veloce Publishing at the above address.
British Library Cataloguing in Publication Data – A catalogue record for this book is available from the British Library. Typesetting, design and page make-up all by Veloce Publishing Ltd on Apple Mac.
Printed and bound by CPI Group (UK) Ltd, Croydon, CR0 4YY.

RALLY GIANTS

Veloce Classic Reprint Series

Toyota Celica GT-Four

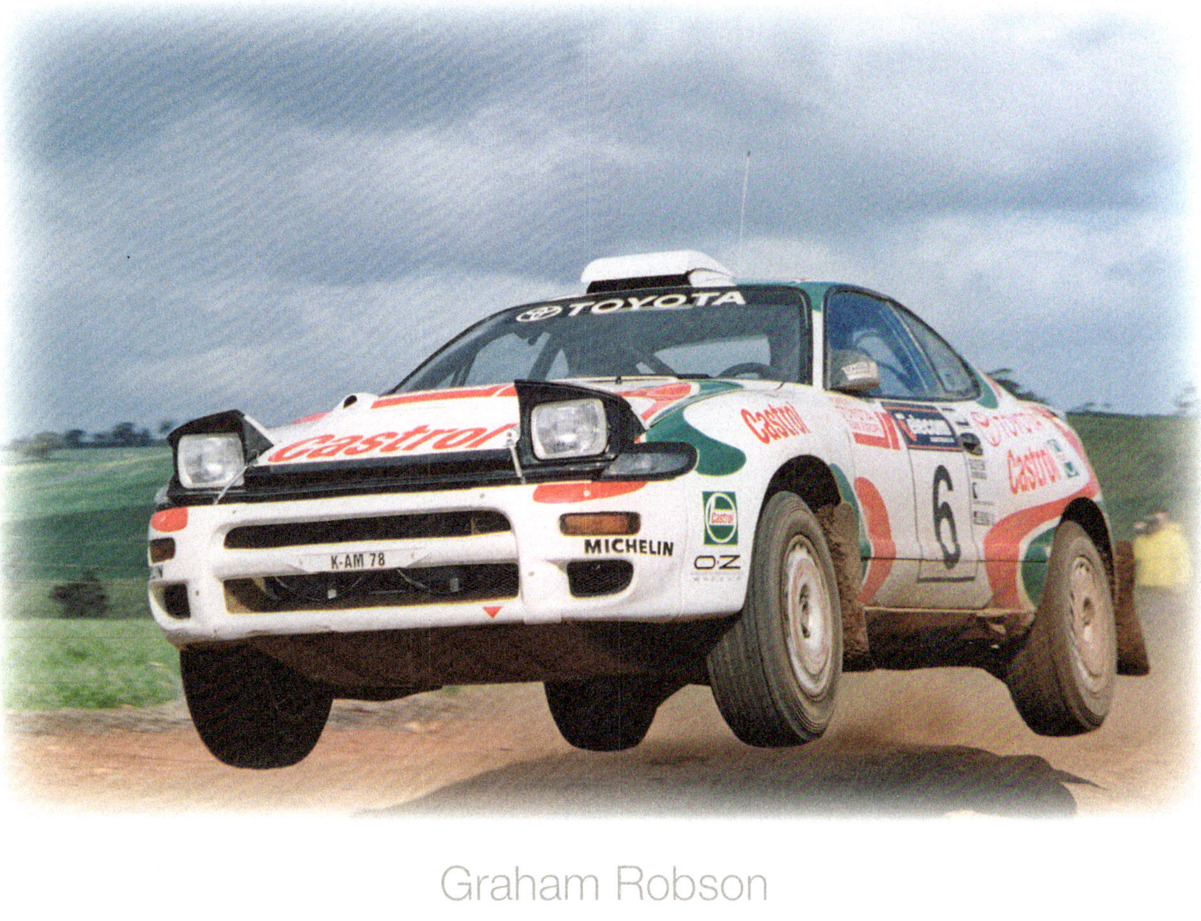

Graham Robson

Contents

Foreword.. 5
Introduction... 7

The car and the team 9
  Inspiration 9
  Toyota Team Europe.. 11
  The Celica GT-Four's importance in rallying 13
  Four-wheel-drive – the breakthrough 14
  Facing up to rival cars.. 15
  Homologation – meeting the rules.......................... 19
  Engineering features 19
  Motorsport development and improvements........... 29
  Building and running the 'works' cars.................... 37
  Who owned who? 38
  Disqualification, and the leaking turbo affair
    of 1995 40
  Personalities and star drivers................................ 43

Competition story 52

The 'works' Celica GT-Four's career 52
  1988 52
  1989 57
  1990 65
  1991 78
  1992 86
  1993 93
  1994 100
  1995 106
  1996 116
  1997 117
  What could succeed the Celica?........................... 118

World/major European rally wins 119

**Works rally cars – World Championship rallies
(and when first used)** 120

Index... 122

Foreword

What is a rally? Today's events, for sure, are completely different from those of a hundred or even fifty years ago. What was once a test of reliability is now a test of speed and strength. What was once a long-distance trial is now a series of short-distance races.

In the beginning, rallying was all about using standard cars in long-distance road events, but by the 1950s the events were toughening up. Routes became rougher, target speeds were raised, point-to-point speed tests on special stages were introduced, and high performance machines were needed to ensure victory.

Starting in the late 1950s, too, teams started to develop extra-special versions of standard cars, which were built in small numbers, and meant only to go rallying, or motor racing. These were the 'homologation specials' which now dominate the sport. The first of these, no question, was the Austin-Healey 3000, and the latest is any one of the ten-off World Rally Cars which we see on our TV screens, or on the special stages of the world.

Although rally regulations changed persistently over the years, the two most important events were four-wheel-drive being authorised from 1979, and the 'World Rally Car'

formula (which required only 20 identical cars to be produced to gain homologation) being adopted in 1997. At all times, however, successful rally cars have needed to blend high performance with strength and reliability.

Unlike Grand Prix cars, they have needed to be built so that major repairs could be carried out at the side of the road, in the dark, sometimes in freezing cold, and sometimes in blazing temperatures.

Over the years, some cars became dominant, only to be eclipsed when new and more advanced rivals appeared. New cars appeared almost every year, but dramatically better machines appeared less often. From time to time, rally enthusiasts would be astonished by a new model, and it was on occasions like that when a new rallying landmark was set.

So, which were the most important new cars to appear in the last half century? What is it that made them special, at the time? In some cases it was perfectly obvious – Lancia's Stratos was the first-ever purpose-built rally car, the Audi Quattro was the first rally-winning four-wheel-drive car, and the Toyota Celica GT-Four was the first rally-winning four-wheel-drive Group A car to come from Japan.

But what about Ford's amazing Escorts? Or the Fiat 131 Abarth? Or the Lancia Delta Integrale? Or, of course, the Subaru Impreza? All of them had something unique to offer, at the time, in comparison with their competitors. Because they offered something different, and raised rallying's standards even further, they were true Rally Giants.

To a rallying petrol-head like me, it would have been easy to choose twenty, thirty or even more rally cars which have made a difference to the sport. However, I have had to be brutal, and cull my list to the very minimum. Listed here in chronological order, these are the 'Rally Giants' cars I have picked out, to tell the on-going story of world-class rallying in the last fifty years:

Car	Period used as a works car
Austin-Healey 3000	1959-1965
Saab 96 and V4	1960-1976
Mini Cooper/Cooper S	1962-1970
Ford Escort Mk I	1968-1975
Lancia Stratos	1974-1981
Ford Escort RS1800	1975-1981
Fiat 131 Abarth	1976-1981
Audi Quattro and S1	1981-1986
Peugeot 205T16	1984-1986
Lancia Delta 4x4/Integrale	1987-1993
Toyota Celica GT-Four	1988-1995
Ford Escort RS Cosworth/WRC	1993-1998
Subaru Impreza Turbo/WRC	1993-2006

There is so much to know, to tell, and to enjoy about each of these cars that I plan to devote a compact book to each one. And to make sure that one can be compared with another, I intend to keep the same format for each volume.

Graham Robson

Introduction

When Toyota turned the pretty Celica GT-Four into a four-wheel-drive rally winner for the 1990s, everyone except their bitterest rivals was delighted. For far too long, it seemed, Toyota's rally team, as run by Ove Andersson's Toyota Team Europe (TTE), had been seen as underdogs.

Although the early Toyotas could be strong and reliable, they were rarely fast enough or special enough to match big-spending rivals of the period, such as Audi, Ford, Lancia and Peugeot. Suddenly, with the arrival of the Celica GT-Four, it seemed that this would change. High technology and the finance to back the cars was available. Game on!

In many ways, though, what followed from 1988, and rumbled on for the next decade, was the growing impression that the team, the cars and what they became were not always as transparent, or as straightforward, as they seemed. Even today, Toyota's disqualification over turbocharger irregularities (in late 1995, which resulted in the team being thrown out of World events for the next full season) is remembered as a most important shadow over an impressive record.

No matter. In almost every other way, the development, and running, of Celica GT-Fours at World rallying level was a triumph of enterprise against all the odds, and of experience against the unlimited funds available to rivals. This was a time when companies like Lancia were spending gazillions on developing the best rally car in the world, and when Ford would take four years in getting the Escort RS Cosworth from 'Great Idea' to homologated use.

Toyota, for its part, had to tackle its future faster, and in a more pragmatic manner. Because Toyota's top management would not sanction work on an entirely fresh and specialised model, TTE had to settle down, to pick up the most suitable car they found in the Japanese giant's diverse range, and to turn it into a competitive rally car. Along the way, Toyota would benefit by becoming the first ever Japanese automotive brand to match the European rally teams in everything they attempted.

For TTE in mid-1986, the future of its rally programme was looking bleak. Because it only had rear-wheel-drive, the team's elephantine old Group B Celica Twin-Cam Turbo was obsolete. To replace it, work had been going ahead for some time on Group B MR2 projects – one car with a mid-mounted/in–line engine, one with a mid-mounted/transverse-engine, but *both* with four-wheel-drive. The FIA (the sport's all-powerful organising body) then proposed a new and ultra-specialised 'Group S' formula, at which point the MR2s had to become potential Group S projects instead. Finally, in a shattering blow, which was precipitated by poor Henri Toivonen's crash in Corsica in May 1986, the FIA suddenly killed off Group B *and* Group S, and imposed Group A instead.

Whether Toyota liked it or not (and TTE, make no mistake, did *not* like it …), to stay in World rallying in the late 1980s/early 1990s they would now have to develop a Group A car with four-wheel-drive and at least 300bhp. Ove Andersson was summoned to Japan, shown a complete product plan for Toyota's future, and was told that he could develop only one of the cars that were already listed therein.

Although Ove Andersson later said up to that time he had not previously considered turning the just announced Celica GT-Four into a competitive Group A car, along with his colleagues at TTE he then carried out a splendid development, evolution, and rally car honing job on the basic four-wheel-drive car which was available. It was to TTE's enormous credit that it turned an outwardly un-promising car into a World rally winner in little more than a year's competition. For this, although Ove believed in running TTE as a real team effort, with few prima donnas, he was always ready to give much credit to Karl-Heinz Goldstein's engineering skills, along with those of the Xtrac four-wheel-drive system for turning the still raw GT-Four into a competitive Group A machine.

For the next five years one or other of the GT-Four models became one of the true Rally Giants of the period, even though this was the period in which Lancia's high spending and always ambitious programme with Delta Integrales tended to overshadow every rival's efforts. First of all, TTE succeeded in making the original GT-Four Type ST165 into a very strong rally car, after which they made the entire package more, and yet more sophisticated, competitive and more capable of tackling all types of event.

Andersson's true genius, however, came when he persuaded a remarkably talented Spaniard, Carlos Sainz, to join the team. It was Carlos who completed the job of turning a potential winner into a *real* winner, all the way up to World Championship levels. Sainz, the compulsive tester with unearthly skills, and a *real* hunger for motorsport, was the catalyst which seemed to make all things possible.

Even so, Andersson's finest achievement was probably in being able to minimise the direct Japanese influence over his rally car programme. Although Toyota always spent a high proportion of their funds on the East African Safari Rally (with justification – the Celica GT-Four cars won that gruelling event five times), they indulged Andersson in the rest of his programme. As the years passed by, and different model ranges (the ST185 and then the ST205) were introduced, the Japanese also tried to add specially requested features, which certainly enhanced the rally cars' behaviour.

Above all, this is the story of how one basic motor car – all types shared the same basic structural platform, engine and four-wheel-drive transmission – was evolved from a rather anaemic road car to a fire breathing rally car of the very highest standard, and kept at the forefront of motorsport for nearly a decade. Along the way, there were many victories to be celebrated, a number of disappointments and – yes it must be admitted – a number of scandals to be faced.

In every way, however, the Celica GT-Four was a much-respected rally car that many enthusiasts remember with great joy – and this, I hope, is the complete story of its turbulent career.

Graham Robson

The car and the team

Inspiration

Although this story begins with four-wheel-drive – the first four-wheel-drive range of cars to be engineered by Toyota – this layout was not inspired by the need to go rallying. Indeed, if Audi had not introduced the four-wheel-drive Quattro as a road car in 1980, I doubt if other four-wheel-drive cars would have appeared in such profusion at this time.

Time, then, for a very brief history lesson. The very first Toyota Celica was a conventional front-engine/rear-drive sports coupé, announced at the end of 1970, and almost instantly a success. Within two years Toyota was producing more than 150,000 Celicas every year (with more than half of these cars being delivered in North America). Once the relentless march of Japanese technology got into gear, and the four-cylinder Celica was joined by the closely related six-cylinder Supra, Toyota wondered why and how it could ever have managed without this range of sporting cars.

One thing led to another. A second-generation Celica, with totally new styling, came along in 1977, a third-generation (new styling again) followed in 1981, but all these cars adopted the same, conventional, format of a front-mounted, in-line engine driving the rear wheels. Then came the truly revolutionary change, inspired by Toyota's intention to promote a more high tech image – not only was the fourth-generation Celica of 1985 a transverse-engined/front-wheel-drive car, but a four-wheel-drive derivative was also planned.

Ove Andersson, founder, boss, and inspiration behind TTE, knew everything, and was everywhere – it would have been unthinkable to see this team trying to run without him. (Courtesy Phil Short)

This is how the Celica rally story really began, when Ove Andersson drove a 1600GT in 1973. Here he is, taking twelfth place, in the RAC Rally.

The inspiration, therefore, came from two major sources – one was that the motoring world – outside North America at least – had definitely concluded that transversely-mounted engines with front-wheel-drive were the most efficient way of packaging a mass production car, while the Quattro (and especially its rally successes) had inspired other companies to try out four-wheel-drive for themselves.

There was nothing new about front-wheel-drive, of course, for Citroën, DKW and Saab had produced FWD cars years before Alec Issigonis's legendary Mini hit the streets.

The idea of a transversely-mounted four-cylinder engine, on the other hand, was a real Mini novelty when it appeared in 1959. It was only when rival car makers analysed the layout, crunched their numbers regarding costs, packaging, and handling, that the idea of a transverse-engine/integral transmission package became popular. First of all it was Fiat, then Renault, then VW which established a trend in Europe. As far as I can see, Datsun was the first Japanese brand to join the party, but once Toyota joined in, with its middle-size cars, there was a rush to conform.

Toyota Team Europe

By 1972, the Swedish driver Ove Andersson was an acknowledged Scandinavian rallying superstar. Having already driven factory cars for Saab, Lancia, Ford and Alpine-Renault, he had won at world level on several occasions, including the Monte Carlo and Acropolis events.

Ove first drove a Celica in that year, and it was only months before Toyota helped him set up a 'works' team in Sweden which, in the beginning, only had four mechanics. From 1975, however, he set up Toyota Team Europe (TTE) at a modest base in Brussels, Belgium, moved the operation to Cologne, Germany four years later, and saw it grow, and become ever more successful in the years that followed.

The original programme was tightly financed, and modestly promoted, so initial entries were made in rear-drive Corolla and Celica GTs. The first 2OHC 2.0-litre rally cars were entered in 1975, a 16-valve version of that engine was adopted soon afterwards, but this was then killed off by an FIA change of regulations. For the next two years the team struggled with engines which were not competitive against Ford's Escort RS1800 and Fiat's 131 Abarth, but things bucked up again when a 16-valve engine was re-homologated at the end of 1979, though victories were very rare.

When Group B rallying came along from 1982, TTE asked the Japanese for a four-wheel-drive car (this was rather premature, as is now clear), but instead were offered a car originally badged as a Celica GT-T, which was a 2-litre front-engined/rear-drive. The 'T' stood for turbocharged, the 20-off evolution version of the model (as used by TTE from 1983) became known as the Celica Twin-Cam Turbo, and 'works' cars eventually produced 370bhp – but always struggled for grip.

Although Toyota eventually began to develop a four-wheel-drive MR2-based car (in great secrecy), it was the Twin-Cam Turbo which did so much for TTE's reputation in the mid-1980s. The first outright victory came in the Ivory Coast Rally (in West Africa) in October 1983, and was followed by more wins in the Safari of 1984, 1985 and 1986, plus the Ivory Coast of 1985 and 1986. After this car was banned from competition, there was then a short period in which TTE used old-style front-engine/rear-drive Supras and Supra Turbos in long-distance events, but henceforth the principal effort went into the evolution of the Celica GT-Four and all its future developments.

The story of TTE in the late 1980s and most of the 1990s was totally bound up in the GT-Fours, but after the scandal of 'cheating' turbochargers (which caused TTE to be banned from World rallying for the whole of 1996), work went ahead on the engineering of the 20-off Corolla World Rally Car. After further successes had been gained with this compact new machine, Toyota decided that its motorsport future ought to be in Formula One, which meant that the rally team closed down completely at the end of the 1990s.

Once Toyota had adopted transverse-engined/integral transmission packaging, it was almost inevitable that these should be adopted on sporting machinery. Amazingly, though, the original derivative – the MR2 – featured the engine/transmission package, but mounted *behind* the seats, and driving the rear wheels. The fourth-generation Celica, however, had its power pack up front, driving the front wheels, this all being 'lifted,' in modified form, from the latest Corona/Carina family car.

That, therefore, was the inspiration behind the layout of the fourth-generation Celica – but the *real* inspiration behind the development of the four-wheel-drive Celica GT-Four came from a single source – that of the Audi Quattro. Launched in March 1980, the Quattro went on sale before the end of that year, and it started an illustrious rallying career in January 1981. Once it started winning at World level, there were several initial victories in 1981, and many more in the years that followed.

The Quattro's influence on the world of motoring should never be underestimated. Once its rally successes had started to roll, and Audi's four-wheel-drive system had been promised for other models too, the rest of the world sat up, took interest, and started thinking about their own future. It was no coincidence that one of the first Ford Sierra-based concept cars was to have had four-wheel-drive, but as soon as Ford bosses grasped the significance of the Quattro, that concept car was hastily put back behind closed doors, and the XR4x4 was developed.

This was the point at which both Toyota and Lancia committed themselves to producing four-wheel-drive derivatives of still-secret new models (Celica and Lancia Delta, respectively) – but it is worth noting that, at that point, neither had any intention of committing such new-type production cars to a motorsport development programme.

Even before the Celica GT-Four was announced, by the mid-1980s Toyota had been well-advanced with the design and development of a new Group B/Group S car – four-wheel-drive turbocharged versions of the MR2, of which several progressively more advanced prototypes had been built. Because of this, and the related investment costs and engineering efforts involved, neither Toyota nor its rallying arm, Toyota Team Europe, was at all interested in the Celica GT-Four.

It was only the abrupt cancellation of Group B rallying – the announcement came in mid-1986 – that caused companies who were seriously committed to world rallying to look around, and to see which

In recent years, Toyota has occasionally displayed the stillborn Type 222D Group S MR2s, in transverse-engine (left) or in-line engine (right) form.

Once the Group S MR2 project had been cancelled in 1986, TTE put the surviving cars in store in Cologne. Here they are, tucked away among a number of other intriguing cars in the company's racing and rally collection.

Two distinctly different mechanical layouts of Group S MR2 car were tried in 1985/1986 – this being the in-line engine application, with a special type of four-wheel-drive transmission.

The second of the MR2 222D Group S projects featured a transversely-mounted 2-litre engine. Note the absolutely huge turbocharger – so estimates of 600bhp were probably close to the mark!

other models could be pressed into service in the new, post-Group B, environment. Because the new regulations specified Group A cars which, by definition, had to be built in quantities of at least 5000 in a year of production, a great deal of thought – at boardroom and marketing department levels – had to take place, and some companies took longer than others to make decisions, and to prepare new rally cars.

For the record, Toyota (the business, that is, not Toyota Team Europe) had started work on the fourth-generation Celica GT, the first to have front-wheel-drive, in 1983, launching it at the end of 1985. Work on the four-wheel-drive derivative, the GT-Four, had started at the same time, but took longer to bring to fruition – this important new car being previewed in 1985, but properly introduced on 1 October 1986.

The Celica GT-Four's importance in rallying

For Toyota, the introduction of a new medium-sized four-wheel-drive Group A car into rallying was important at all levels – not merely so that TTE could use it as a 'works' car at World level, but so that supported or purely private owners and teams all over the world could also take advantage of its qualities – traction, performance and typically-Japanese high levels of build quality and engineering excellence.

When one surveyed the rally scene in the late 1980s, the arrival of a credible new car such as the GT-Four was important, for it instantly provided much more choice in the rallying marketplace. At first, after Group B (200-off, and 20 Evolution cars) was killed off, and Group A (5000-off, and no allowance for limited-production evolution types) took its place at the end of 1986, there was very little choice of fully-developed four-wheel-drive cars. Toyota, for instance, was obliged to run massive 3-litre-engined Supras, which were competitive in rough and tough endurance events like the Safari, and the Ivory Coast, but hopeless in European 'sprint' events.

In the first 'Group A' season – 1987 – Lancia's Delta HF4x4 was the only competitive four-wheel-drive car in the field, for Ford's Sierra XR4x4 was under-powered and too heavy, as were the Audi 200 Turbo and Coupé Quattro (normally-aspirated) types, while Mazda's 323 4WD was a 1.6-litre-engined car. Although Ford's Sierra RS Cosworth and BMW's M3 were very fast cars (and supreme on the race tracks of the world), they lacked four-wheel-drive, which was vital for loose-surface rallying. Although Lancia originally claimed a mere 240bhp from its turbocharged 2-litre engine (this was almost certainly underestimated), it was quite enough at first.

A year later, 1988, with the Celica GT-Four ready to join the world rally 'circus,' the Lancia had become the Delta Integrale, with 280bhp, Mitsubishi had also launched the four-wheel-drive 290bhp Galant VR4, but that was about the height of it all. Until, and unless, Ford (whose turbocharged YB engine was certainly the most powerful) could bring a four-wheel-drive Sierra Cosworth to market, Lancia was still the main opposition – and the Delta was about to be made more formidable with the launch of the 300bhp-plus 16-valve derivative.

Accordingly, the arrival of the GT-Four (even with a claimed 265bhp – another figure which may have been accurate at first, but which soon became irrelevant, one is certain) was very important, for it immediately threatened to provided a real counterbalance to the dominant Lancia team. More important, and as far as Oriental 'face' was concerned, it showed every sign of being Japan's first successful Group A car, for it was at once more nimble, lighter, and backed by more sheer rally expertise than was the Mitsubishi Galant VR4.

Although TTE was neither interested nor capable of flooding the market with works-specification cars (Lancia was a past master at this tactic, while companies like Ford were always willing to provide mountains of special competition parts to allow private owners to build their own replicas), they would gradually make sure that national teams – notably those in Sweden and Belgium – soon had sold-off ex-works cars to carry on the good work. It meant that from 1979 onwards, there would be more and more competition Celica GT-Fours in entry lists.

Four-wheel-drive – the breakthrough

If it had not been for Audi's rallying success with the Quattro, four-wheel-drive rally cars might not have appeared at all until late in the 1980s. However, and as has already become clear in other volumes in the *Rally Giants* series, Audi's motorsport victories were followed by those of Peugeot (with the Group B 205 Turbo 16), and Lancia with a series of Delta-based cars – the Group B S4 and the Group A Delta HF4x4/Integrale-types. By this time, in any case, a four-wheel-drive chassis layout had come to appeal to the marketing staffs of companies all around the world, and when Ford adopted it for their Sierra XR4x4, it was certain that the message had got through, even at mass-market level.

Until 1979, international FIA regulations specifically banned four-wheel-drive cars from going rallying. Almost

Years before the Celica GT-Four was even conceived, TTE was battling to win events with older, rear-drive, Celicas; this is Björn Waldegård on the 1981 Acropolis Rally.

immediately the occasional Range Rover, and desperately under-powered Subarus, then appeared in truly rough-road African events before Audi suddenly launched the 200bhp Quattro in 1980: once homologated, the Quattro started winning in 1981, and came to dominate World rallying in the next three years. As I make clear later in this section, Toyota was well-advanced with the development of a new Group B/Group S MR2 in 1986, but when Group B was cancelled, that decision left it in the lurch. Like other manufacturers – not least Ford and General Motors – competitions managers woke up the morning after that decision, to see their forward programmes in disarray.

If Toyota was to stay in rallying, and as with rivals such as Lancia, and Ford, the search for a four-wheel-drive car had to be made in a hurry, and as with the rivals, the available choice was not widespread. The Supras were fast, but available only with rear-wheel-drive. As confirmed by Ove Andersson in later years: "The Celica GT-Four was never intended to go into motorsport. When we knew that the car would have to be used for rallying, it was too late to have any influence on the design. However, we have many notebooks full of changes we would want to make for the next version …"

As far as Toyotas and TTE were concerned, the timetable of what had already happened, and what would eventually happen, tells a fascinating story:

1982: Styling work on a fourth-generation Celica began.
1983: Engineering work on new-generation transverse-engined Celicas began.
August 1985: Introduction of a new transverse-engined front-wheel-drive Celica GT.
May 1986: Group B/Group S rally category killed off, effective 31 December 1986. All previous work on still-secret Toyota MR2 therefore nullified.
1 October 1986: Introduction of four-wheel-drive Celica GT-Four.
1 January 1987: World rallying henceforth to be run to Group A regulations.
1 May 1988: Celica GT-Four gained Group A homologation. TTE entries in motorsport began at once.

It was the foundation of a sturdy development programme that would see the Celica, and developments of that first design, become potential World rally winners for the next decade. By any standards, therefore, the GT-Four was a Rally Giant.

Facing up to rival cars

When the first Group A four-wheel-drive Toyota Celica was conceived, because no behind-the-scenes motorsport development had yet been done, TTE needed to get it ready in a great hurry. Several years had already been lost – first of all by the Toyota parent company insisting that the unwieldy rear-wheel-drive Celica Twin-Cam Turbo be used in Group B, then by the abortive MR2 Group B project, which had had to be killed off by the abrupt cancellation of Group B.

By mid-1986, prototypes of the Group B MR2 had been built (some with transversely-mounted engines behind the two-seater cabin, some with in-line engines), and since at least three of these cars survive (they are occasionally seen at classic rally car events in Europe), we can still see how far TTE and Toyota had progressed in their thinking about four-wheel-drive and turbocharged engine technology.

Coded 222D, these MR2 project cars looked superficially like original-style MR2s, but were totally different under the skin. Apart from the turbocharged 2.0-litre engine configuration, rear-wheel-drive and four-wheel-drive (by XTrac) were already being assessed. The engine itself was a typically state-of-the-art Toyota power unit, with twin-plug heads, four valves per cylinder, turbocharging, and the target (which might indeed have been achieved in due course) of 600bhp.

[If this sounds extreme, it should be made clear that in 1986, existing Group B cars – Lancia Delta S4, Peugeot 205 T16 and Ford RS200 – all had up to 500bhp, and each team was planning big power increases for 1987 and beyond – the 'rallycross' 2.1-litre RS200s eventually had a reliable 650bhp.]

After Group B was cancelled by the authorities, it

In the early 1980s, Toyota developed the limited production Celica Twin-Cam Turbo for Group B motorsport. With no less than 370bhp, it was formidable on rough and tough endurance events, but lacked four-wheel-drive.

was immediately clear that there was going to be a world of difference between the development of an ultra-special 200-off Group B car (like the MR2 was shaping up to be), and that of a 5000-off 'homologation special' Group A car. Even so, just as soon as TTE team boss Ove Andersson learned that Group B had no future, he began the patient lobbying needed for 5000 four-wheel-drive cars to be built: Toyota would have to guarantee a full development programme and lay down dedicated assembly facilities in

When Toyota designed a Group B car in the early 1980s, TTE boss Ove Andersson requested four-wheel-drive, but this was refused. The rear-drive Celica Twin-Cam Turbo of the 1983-1986 period was a very effective interim car instead.

Japan. Ove was pushing at an open door – this, in fact, was already under way.

The line up of rallying rivals changed significantly – and intensified, of course – in the 1986-1988 period, so Toyota had to plan ahead, and be ambitious. There would be no point in trying to produce a new car to match the 1986-vintage opposition and those already known to be on the stocks, for within two years other rival machines would surely have appeared.

When the Celica GT-Four programme was confirmed, the dominant competitor was certain to be the Lancia Delta HF4x4 – though at the time no-one realised that this would become the Delta Integrale very shortly afterwards – and almost all the other brands would be playing catch-up. This, therefore, is a listing of what cars Toyota would have to beat in the next few years, and it is important to realise that not all of them had four-wheel-drive:

BMW M3 – front-engine, rear-wheel-drive. Newly-launched in 1986, a dedicated Group A car, principally intended for touring car racing. Carefully engineered, but hampered by two features – it only had rear-wheel-drive, and used a normally-aspirated 2.3-litre engine. BMW was not really interested in rallying, yet the British Prodrive organisation produced competitive M3s for tarmac events: wisely, loose-surface events were ignored. A winner in Corsica in 1987, but nowhere else, the M3 soon stepped down to European-level competition. Glittering success was achieved, all over the world, on the race track. Four-wheel-drive versions were never developed.

Ford Sierra RS Cosworth – front-engine, rear-wheel-drive. Having lost the use of the Group B RS200, this was Ford's 'default' competition car for the immediate future, but rear-wheel-drive was always to be a problem. With 300bhp-plus, it was enormously fast on good tarmac, but always struggled on low-friction surfaces – the result being only one World victory (Corsica 1988). Too big and too heavy, it gave rise to the Sierra Cosworth 4x4 of 1990, but that car was also too heavy, and three years too late to be a winner. Closely related to the Sierra XR4x4.

Ford Sierra XR4x4 – front-engine, four-wheel-drive. If only … if only … if only this car had had 300bhp instead of 210bhp (the asthmatic 2.8-litre V6 could produce no more), it might have been a winner in 1987 and 1988. Equipped with the four-wheel-drive that the faster Sierra RS Cosworth lacked, and much heavier, it was a good 'place' car, and useful in European events, but not at World level.

Lancia Delta HF4x4 and Integrale – front transverse-engine, four-wheel-drive. The established long-term favourite, with a success record beginning in January 1987, when it was still the less-powerful Delta HF4x4. As the improved, 300bhp, Integrale from 1988, it became a multiple World Champion for Lancia, and for the lucky drivers hired to use it. Perhaps a touch small, and lacking in wheel movement, it was powerful, the lightest, most nimble, and best financed of all. With generous 'works' support, it would be Toyota's biggest rival to the end of 1992, then rapidly fall away.

Mazda 323 4WD – front transverse-engine, four-wheel-drive. Only competitive because it was launched at the very beginning of the Group A era, this Mazda was neither powerful enough, strong enough, nor seriously supported by the factory, to make much impact on World Rallying. First of all there had been a 323 Turbo, with 175bhp and front-wheel-drive, which was unsuccessful as there were persistent transmission breakages. The 4WD version of 1986 and 1987 had 240bhp and 1.6 litres, but in spite of attracting drivers like Hannu Mikkola and Timo Salonen, was not good enough to win World Rallies, though seconds and thirds were recorded.

For 1990 the 323 GTX took over, with 1.8 litres/300bhp, but it was still not a pace-setter. Cars like the Toyota Celica GT-Four and the Lancia Delta Integrale eventually humiliated it, and the cars would be withdrawn in 1992.

Mitsubishi Galant VR4 – front transverse-engine, four-wheel-drive. With four-wheel-steering, it would be homologated in 1988. Too big and too heavy to beat Toyota (and Lancia) on a regular basis, it was competitive when stars such as Ari Vatanen, Pentti Airikkala and Mikael Ericsson drove the 'works' cars, and there were occasional World victories. Important because the engine, transmission and basic know-how would all be used in the much lighter and smaller Lancer RS which followed in 1993 – every driver hated the four-wheel-steering of the Galant, which was therefore abandoned.

Team driver Tommi Makinen (signed for 1995 and later seasons) went on to dominate World Rallying in the Lancer Evo series, taking the Drivers' Championship in four successive years.

Homologation – meeting the rules

Unlike the methods which had to be used by Toyota's rivals – notably Lancia, which only got the Delta HF4x4 homologated by using two different types of turbocharger, and Ford which used two different types of fuel-injection on the Sierra XR4x4, to make up the numbers – the Japanese concern never had any trouble with meeting the regulations.

To qualify for Group A homologation, Toyota had to guarantee that it had built more than 5000 examples of the Celica GT-Four, Type ST165. By 1987, Celica GT production was in such profusion that 118,000 cars would be built in that year. All Celicas, whether front-wheel-drive or four-wheel-drive, were built in the same factory in Japan – and, as we now know, more than 90 per cent of these cars were exported, the lion's share going to the USA. No accurate breakdown of GT-Four assembly has been released by Toyota, but even if only five per cent of all those cars were GT-Fours, the 5000-plus total must easily have been achieved.

By comparison, Ford had to struggle (successfully) to build 5000 of the very special Sierra RS Cosworth before the end of 1986, while Lancia's Delta HF4x4 claims for production numbers were originally suspect (though demand for the later Integrales, either of the 8V and 16V variety, was always considerably higher).

Although the original GT-Four was not homologated until 1 May 1988 (just, and only just, in time for the first TTE cars to start the Tour de Corse), sufficient cars were certainly produced in 1987 for this date to have been advanced by several months. TTE, it seems, was in no hurry, however, as it wanted to complete development of some special Group A components before photographs had to be taken for inclusion in the Homologation Form.

TTE had the same relaxed experience in achieving Group A homologation without hassle on the ST185 and ST205-types (even though both of those cars were built in specially-developed 'limited edition' versions of the originals), principally because it never rushed to get new-shape cars into rallying until they had been on the market for some time.

Engineering features
Original GT-Four Road Car (Type ST165)

First of all there was the Celica of the 1970s, a very simply engineered sporty coupé with a front-engine and rear-wheel-drive, originally developed in Japan for Toyota to sell in the USA. After great commercial success with three generations of such cars, Toyota then introduced a new fourth-generation Celica GT in 1985, with a new layout.

Based on the expensively-developed engineering of the latest Corona/Camry saloons, and other related mid-sized Toyotas, the new car featured transversely-mounted engines, a gearbox mounted alongside those engines, and front-wheel-drive. By the time the range was fully launched, there was a choice of coupé or convertible styles, 1.6, 1.8, and 2.0-litre engines, and a five-speed manual or fully automatic transmission – though no four-wheel-drive at first.

As shared with other front-wheel-drive Corona/Carina-types, there were three new basic examples of four-cylinder engines, but as far as the enthusiastic driver (and, in fact, the rally competitor) was concerned, the most important in the original line-up was the 3S-GELU power unit, which was a 16-valve, 2ohc, 1998cc four-cylinder unit with 86mm bore *and* stroke dimensions. This normally-aspired engine produced a rousing 160bhp at 6400rpm.

All the basics were present for a four-wheel-drive version to be developed, though there was little evidence, at first, of that being one of Toyota's intentions. The basic chassis was very suitably laid out – there was independent suspension by MacPherson at the front and rear, along with power-assisted rack-and-pinion steering, four-wheel disc brakes, and cast-alloy wheels, though if there was any disappointment for motorsport tuners, it was that the cars ran on 14in-diameter road wheels. (According to homologation rules, this meant the rally cars could use up to 16in-diameter wheels, but that was the authorised limit.)

The body style featured a sloping nose, complete with pop-up headlamps, and the coupé had 2+2 seating, the cabin being large enough for the dimensions to easily meet all of the space requirements of Group A homologation.

As introduced in 1986/1987, the original GT-Four Road Car looked smooth and understated. No wonder Ove Andersson always insisted there had originally been no thought of using it as a competition car.

A hatchback was standard on the closed car and from 1987 there would also be a convertible too.

Outsiders, of course, already knew that, at that stage, a four-wheel-drive version of this new car – which we would soon know as the Celica GT-Four – was also under development, for a prototype had been shown at the Frankfurt Motor Show in September 1985 – though with no introduction date promised. Simply, four-wheel-drive had become very fashionable in the early 1980s, especially as the Audi Quattro had become so successful both in motorsport and in the showrooms of the world.

At first (in the same instance of serendipity as the Lancia Delta HF4x4/Integrale) Toyota did not apparently intend this as a competition car, but the sudden cancellation of

This was the first of the transverse-engined/front-wheel-drive Celicas, as introduced in 1985. A four-wheel-drive version, the Celica GT-Four, was already under development and would follow in 1986.

Group B motorsport in mid-1986 (which effectively killed off the Group B/Group S MR2 project) made it viable. Compared with the front-wheel-drive cars, the four-wheel-drive GT-Four (which many enthusiasts now know by its internal code number, ST165) was at once very similar looking, but was mechanically different under the skin. Naturally, the pressed-steel platform had needed to be re-engineered, to accommodate the front-to-rear propeller shaft: allowance for this had been made, right from the start of design and engineering work.

Officially launched in this model in October 1986, the 1998cc engine was now codified as 3S-GTE, and its peak power had been boosted to 185bhp (and the claimed top speed had risen to 140mph, though independent testers thought otherwise). This was achieved not only by having Toyota's own brand of turbocharger (for which Ove Andersson gave grateful thanks, as it clearly offered great potential for the future), but by having a water-cooled intercooler, which most engineers agreed would give even more potential for higher outputs to be gained on competition cars: automatic transmission was not an option on this derivative, and a different type of independent rear suspension (featuring trailing arms and coil springs) was used.

On the road cars, four-wheel-drive was straightforwardly installed by 'growing' a locking centre-diff from a bevel-gear in the original transmission, and providing a 50/50 torque split. The rear differential was carried on a subframe under the modified floor pan/platform, and of course it was the need to accommodate rear driveshafts which had been one reason for altering the rear suspension layout.

According to official figures released by Toyota at the time, the original GT-Four was a whopping 462lb/210kg heavier than the 2-litre front-wheel-drive variety, which sounded excessive for the extra transmission and modified rear suspension which had been added. Not that this worried TTE too much, for once its engineering team tackled a weight reducing programme, the 'works' rally cars were soon shaved down to a competitive level.

Opposite page, top: The GT-Four went on sale in October 1986, originally with a 185bhp engine.

Although this did not apply to the specification of the rally car, the road car was set up with a catalytic converter as standard, and would therefore only run on unleaded fuel – in fact, it was the very first car to be sold in the UK with a converter as standard. British deliveries, incidentally, began early in 1988, when the UK retail price was £20,495. For this, the purchaser got a car with an independently recorded top speed of 135mph, 0-60mph in 7.6 seconds, though because of the extra weight it was carrying (compared with front-driven Celicas) this was not as rapid as originally expected.

Second-generation GT-Four Road Car (ST185-type)

Based on the new fifth-generation Celica, the replacement type of the GT-Four Road Car, the ST185, made its bow, in Japan, at the end of 1989, although the replacement four-wheel-drive car which TTE intended to use in World rallying, a wider-bodied and more specialised type (now called Celica GT-Four A) was not launched until August 1990. The version intended for World Rallying – the GT-Four RC, wide-bodied with many technical improvements, was not launched until September 1991, and did not achieve Group A homologation until January 1992. As far as Toyota was concerned, in Europe this was different enough to be marketed as the 'Carlos Sainz Limited Edition.' In the rallying business, it was always known as the 'Celica Turbo 4WD,' to differentiate it from the original type.

As before, the front-wheel-drive types were available as a complete range with (depending on the market in which the car was to be sold) 1.8 and 2.0 litres, while the 1998cc engine of the new type ST185 GT-Four was originally rated at 225bhp @ 6000rpm in Japan. In the next two years, a special edition type would be launched with 235bhp.

The ST185 took over directly from the ST165, and used the same basic platform and running gear. On the first batch of cars (which TTE did not use as the basis of its rally cars), the only extra air intakes up front were a scoop in the bonnet and small, discreet louvres each side of that scoop.

Opposite page, bottom left and right: This was the fascia/instrument panel/seating arrangement of early Celica GT-Four Road Cars. 'Works' rally cars would look very different!

This carefully posed shot shows how the 'Carlos Sainz' special edition of the ST185 was related to the latest 'works' rally car of the period. To idealise this car for rallying, there were extra fresh air vents in the front bumper moulding, and in the bonnet panel itself.

The style of the new car was much more swoopy and sinuous than the classic shape which it replaced, and it is fair to say that it caused great controversy throughout its life. Much work had gone into optimising engine bay airflow, which explains the use of air extractor vents in the bonnet top, along with more and larger air inlet slots and scoops in the front moulding, to service the cooling radiator, the turbo intercooler and (on rally-prepared cars) the transmission and power-steering coolers too.

Along with the relocation of the turbo intercooler (which was placed horizontally above the engine), TTE claimed this meant that in motorsport the under-bonnet temperature had been reduced from 100°C to around 60°C, which helped translate into an effective increase of more than 40bhp, which could be fed to the transmission.

Although both front-drive and four-wheel-drive types used the same basic chassis platforms as their predecessors, the cabins were new, and weighed little more than before: Toyota claimed that the bodyshells were much more rigid: the fact that the coupés featured more pressed/welded-steel, and less glass, than before no doubt helped. On the GT-Four, the turbocharger was now a dual-entry-type, with two exhaust ports, which effectively meant that the same turbo was separately serving pairs of cylinders.

The balance of the re-engineering of the new four-wheel-drive car was really to update the specification of the earlier car – with bigger brakes, different suspension geometry, and more a rigid body structure. However, much detailed thought had gone into the modernisation, especially on the wide-bodied GT-Four A, where flared front and rear wheelarches allowed for larger wheels, tyres (205/55-15in), brakes and related components to be fitted.

One big advance was that the road cars now ran on 15in wheels. Because FIA Group A regulations only allowed two-inch larger than standard diameter wheels to be homologated for motorsport, this meant that 'tarmac' rally cars could finally use the desirable 17in wheels and Pirelli rubber, and there would be space for larger Group A brakes too.

"We are lucky that so much of the new car is the same as the old one," Ove Andersson stated. "It means we have a chance to develop things like the transmission, which is still a very simple system …"

Even so, Andersson and TTE was in no hurry to change over all its efforts from ST165 (original type) to ST185 (second-type, particularly the wide-bodied variety), and in GT-Four RC form this car would not be phased into motorsport until 1992, though it then had a front line life of three seasons. Not only did this car have a water-cooled engine intercooler, but there were extra cooling vents in the bonnet , a larger bumper cooling intake, and changes to the cylinder head which boosted peak power to 235bhp at 6000rpm.

Toyota set out to make precisely 5000 GT-Four RCs, allocating 1800 examples to the home market – apparently they sold out almost at once, which is a measure of what the TTE rally programme was doing for the company's image. Just 440 'Carlos Sainz' limited edition types were made available in the UK.

Third-generation Road Car (ST205-type)

Like other Japanese manufacturers of the day, Toyota did not keep a model running indefinitely. Toyota-watchers, therefore, were not surprised to see yet another version of the GT-Four, the ST205, launched in February 1994. Although the first rally car versions were shown to the media in March 1994 (even before the Safari Rally, where they were not entered), TTE would not see the car homologated, and put into Group A 'works' action, until Australia in September 1994 (a non-Championship round), then in San Remo in October 1994. It was homologated as the 'Celica GT-Four.'

Once again, the ST205 was an evolutionary development of the ST185 which it replaced completely. The same basic platform/engine/transmission/suspension layout was retained, though front and rear tracks were widened, and road cars had 16in instead of 15in wheel rims. This meant that 18in wheels could be fitted, if necessary, with tarmac/racing tyres on Group A rally cars.

Although the styling theme – a curvaceous 2+2 seater with a hatchback tail – was as before, the entire superstructure was new, in a shape which featured four forward-facing headlamps (the main lamps did not flip up and down, but were always exposed), and with a large transverse rear spoiler, which could be propped up on spacers.

Once again there was a power gain, for the latest 3S-GTE 2-litre was rated at 255bhp @ 6000rpm (with 224lb.ft. of

The ST205 Road Car looked purposeful though, as usual, without livery and extra equipment it appeared positively refined. The GT-Four versions, of course, had the extra air intake in the nose in-between the headlamps, and there was a small direct air intake in the bonnet panel to one side of the usual air access grille.

torque at 4000rpm), thanks to ongoing development work on the turbo itself, on the intercooler, and to the valve timing and camshaft timing. A new-type five-speed manual transmission was fitted to the road cars (although this would have no effect on the Group A rally cars, which continued to use a six-ratio Xtrac installation). For homologation purposes, Toyota produced the WRC model, in the strictly limited quantity of 2500 (2100 of these were to be sold in Japan), which had larger front air intakes, including an extra intake between the main inner headlamps.

Once the 2500 examples had been produced, TTE was no longer concerned with the evolution of final Celicas in future years. Demand for all these cars had been falling for some time, and slipped below 50,000 a year in 1995, before the last new-type Celica of all (with the smart sharp-edged styling theme) made its debut at the end of 1999.

One visual feature of the ST205 was the large transverse rear aerofoil, which was functional at high speeds in providing extra downforce. Look carefully, and it's possible to see that the wing itself is mounted on removable pylons, which allow the section to be brought closer to the hatch lid if necessary. This made interesting differences to the aerodynamic performance, and was homologated so that the change could be effected.

When it took over from the ST185, the new ST205-type was seen to have a totally different cabin and exterior style, including a nose with four fixed headlamps. Front-wheel-drive Celicas of this generation had otherwise smooth noses, but GT-Fours always featured extra air vents in the front shroud, and on the bonnet panel itself.

This study of the standard road car engine bay of the ST205 shows there was very little space for fresh air to circulate.

On the ST205, the vast rear spoiler was standard, but its height varied from market to market. Toyota made sure the spacers which allowed this to be done were homologated!

Motorsport development and improvements

Although Andersson's team was already very experienced in all types of rallying, particularly the rough, tough 'endurance' variety, it was by no means as experienced in evolving high technology new-engineering developments. Accordingly, for the new Celica project, Ove Andersson attracted Karl-Heinz Goldstein (who, typically, for this sport, soon gained the nickname of 'Goldie' ...) to join him from Opel/General Motors, where he had been working for Tony Fall on the still-born Opel Group B/Group S project. Goldstein, who only had about four other design engineers to call upon at first, is now credited with much of the original motorsport layout, design work, and problem solving on the GT-Four programme.

Right from the start, Ove stressed that this was a pragmatic, rather than an idealistic, programme:

"I don't think there is any chance of us getting a car which is designed for motorsport in the way that the Lancia is – maybe a 5 per cent chance – and this Celica has not one thing which I have listed and requested for the production car. Nothing at all."

For 1988, the initial thrust was in getting miles on to the cars, to sort out reliability, and only then to begin looking for the last few per cent of engine power, performance and road-holding. Before homologation was even achieved, the team had been testing 'mules' in Greece, Kenya, Holland, Germany and in Corsica – amassing a total of 25,000 to 30,000km (21,739m). An early problem, which took ages to solve, was in managing the airflow into, around, and out of the engine bay, but back in Japan the 'mainstream' engineers understood those problems, and made sure that they were progressively eased on subsequent models.

Because the Japanese have a policy of not 'losing face' if it can be avoided, Toyota's initial approach to campaigning the four-wheel-drive Celicas was to reveal as little as possible about the cars to the media, and particularly to keep many

Gerhard Pfeiffer (centre, with banana, and affectionately known as 'Pepper') was an important member of the TTE engineering team in the early 1990s. Renowned photographer Reinhard Klein is talking to co-driver Arne Hertz immediately behind him. (Courtesy Phil Short)

of their problems firmly behind closed doors. For pundits, reporters and – later – historians, this made it difficult to spot and track technical trends, though ever-helpful drivers like Waldegård and Kankkunen would occasionally drop comments about the way that the car's handling and general feel was improving from event to event.

The original-for-Corsica 1988 specification included modestly-tuned engines (which had been developed by TTE, along with the Japanese themselves), boosted only to 0.9Bar, and producing about 265bhp – which put them way behind the Lancias and Ford Sierras, both of which had comfortably over 300bhp (though neither liked to admit it to the FIA, who wanted to put a cap on rally car performance …). Although the engines were built in Germany, the specification was settled in Japan, where further testing and development was already taking place.

The special six-speed Xtrac transmission (which had been worked up between Goldstein, and Mike Endean of Xtrac) was still in an 'in-progress' specification (only one set of ratios had been homologated at first), and was normally set to provide a 50%F/50%R torque split. Driver-operated controls inside the cabin allowed the central viscous coupling controls to be varied. Because the engines eventually became brutally powerful, the durability of this four-wheel-drive installation was a serious issue.

In 1988 Toyota generously provided this excellent colour cut-away drawing of the ST165 in its original format, complete with Pirelli and Duckhams support decals. Later rally cars would run with the headlamps permanently erect, which may have slightly marred their lines, but helped channel more fresh air into the well-filled engine bay.

This posed testing shot (no engine undershield as far as one can see!) shows off the purposeful lines of the ST165. That vehicle identity – K-AM1422 – does not seem to have been used on any 'works' car which appeared in a World Championship Rally.

In Corsica, the cars had lightened suspension uprights, and were fitted with a front bumper that included no fewer than six extra forward-facing driving lamps – all this on an event where there was virtually no night time motoring! As it happened, and compared with the opposition, the cars were noticeably off the pace, though great to look at, and looking very capable.

The first major development hang-up came in Greece, only the car's second event, where Xtrac-equipped cars (not only Toyota, but Mazda and Opel, too) all suffered in the heat and dust of Greece. Broken planetary gears, dust getting in to the hydraulics, and other control mechanism failures both intervened, so a speedy re-design was needed, and was promised for the 1000 Lakes Rally in August.

Although for 1989 the team was still as secretive as ever regarding specifications, and improvements, there were important advances. The cars, for sure, were not light – an average start-line figure being about 1250kg/2756lb, which was significantly more than that of the standard-setting Lancia Delta Integrales. Carbon-fibre propeller shafts and lighter suspension components were all added to the specification. One important chassis advance was that the team began using water-cooled brakes, and there was continuous work on handling and road-holding throughout the season.

It soon became abundantly clear that there was much more power available than the 'official' 265bhp of 1988 –

Time for a rebuild of the rear axle/rear suspension of a TTE ST165. This service shot was taken on the Monte Carlo Rally. (Courtesy Phil Short)

the Portugal cars, for instance, had 295bhp – and that Carlos Sainz, who liked to test more assiduously than most of his peers, made a very significant contribution. One of his most obvious influences was to persuade Toyota to get rid of the phalanx of permanently-fixed forward-facing driving lamps, which were not needed in daylight rallies, and which were really useless and heavy appendages: the first 'nude' Celicas rallied in Corsica in May.

TTE, however, was always reluctant to share its technical advances with the world, which meant that the media (and, eventually, the sport's historians) found this intensely irritating. This was policy imposed from above, by Toyota bureaucrats in Japan, so although personal relations between Ove Andersson and the media were always amicable, there were signs of strain. Towards the end of the year, more than one rally pundit called this approach 'counter-productive.' Perhaps Toyota could not see this coming – but when certain controversies built up in future seasons, regarding dubious fuel additives, and a rather free interpretation of homologation rules, TTE would find it difficult to keep the media on side …

For 1990 and 1991, new regulations meant that all Group A cars, including the Celicas, had to run with 40mm diameter restrictors positioned upstream of the turbocharger inlets. Since TTE blandly claimed no change to the 'official' power output – 265bhp at 6800rpm – we may never know if the power of this four-cylinder engine had been reduced: the subjective evidence, though, was that peak power might be down, but mid-range and transient torque was significantly increased. Early in the year, the Celicas still ran with fixed headlamps mounted way down in the front grille, but from the Safari onwards, this all changed.

To quote that seasoned observer, Martin Holmes:

"FISA ordered that last year's [1989] headlamp arrangement (in which the headlamps were kept in the down position, but units placed in special places at each side of the grille) should be abandoned. To avail themselves of the rule that headlamp movement mechanism could be removed, the team preferred instead to keep them erect (suffering the increased drag) – but not always – taking advantage of the increased inlet space for cooling air …"

TTE always claimed that it needed every possible concession to allow it to get air into, round and through the engine bay, and there were those observers who claimed to have seen lightweight bonnet panels actually distorting under the pressure of air. "We have been accused of wrongly tampering with these bonnets, and it's quite unfair," Ove Andersson later commented. "In reality this is evidence of our trouble, because it shows the air builds up inside the engine area – even in front of the radiator – and can't otherwise get out …"

Even though the original-shape ST165 car had already become obsolete in 'showroom' terms, TTE used it throughout 1991, and completed more detail work on the specification – though, clearly, much of the effort at Cologne was being concentrated on behind-the-scenes development of the next-generation (ST185) models. As already noted, in homologated condition, by this time the cars usually ran with their headlamp pods erect (even in broad, sunny, daylight), and more fresh air entered the engine bay by that route.

Team boss Ove Andersson was realistic about the car. When interviewed in mid-1991, he admitted that: "There is not a lot left to come. Maybe we can still improve the brakes and road-holding, but in small degrees."

Pirelli always provided the very latest in tyres (amazingly Lancia, Toyota's big rivals, were running on Michelin tyres, and since both Lancia and Pirelli were Italian, this always felt strange …). As time progressed, however, Michelin's big advantage was in developing 'mousse technology,' which allowed rally cars to coninue driving even though their tyres had suffered impact punctures, and for a time Pirelli could not match this. Pirelli's response was to make its rally tyres stronger, and there were sometimes advantages to that, especially on hot events like the Acropolis and the Safari, but they had to change their view when it became clear that a Lancia with a puncture in a 'mousse' Michelin could still achieve competitive times.

This was the one big reason why a change was made at TTE for 1993. In 1992 the change of allegiances was slightly hinted at, for after Marlboro, the cigarette company, arrived

Time for discussion over a tyre choice in mid-event, with Maurice Guaslard (in TTE jacket) taking the tough decisions. (Courtesy Phil Short)

as major sponsor, the name of 'Pirelli' disappeared completely from the front-end colour scheme of the TTE machines, and was carried on the rear bumper moulding instead.

To idealise the cars' suspension they were provided with front and rear anti-roll bars which could be adjusted from the driver's seat by levers mounted on the floorpan close to the gear lever itself. Engine bay cooling continued to be marginal (especially in hot-climate events), but most of the team's efforts to find ways of channelling more air in from the outside world was frustrated by zealous, nit-picking scrutineers.

In 1992 the big change came – that the old ST165-type car was replaced by the new-shape ST185 model, a car which retained much of the same running gear, four-wheel-drive layout, and chassis/platform, but which had a new rounded (and as it transpired) much stiffer coupé bodyshell. Although the engine turbo restrictor regulation was changed yet again – the maximum diameter was set at 38mm from 1 January – it seemed to make little difference to any of the front line cars in the sport. Homologation was achieved on 1 January 1992, which meant that the new-type car could be used throughout the 1992 season: as with the ST165 variety, the new car invariably ran with its fold-down headlamps erect, which rather spoiled the sleek body lines.

As several observers pointed out, then and later, the ST185 was one of the most difficult challenges for TTE to achieve a successful set-up, and it was one (but not the critical) reason why Carlos Sainz left the team at the end of the 1992 season, and why Markku Alen achieved so little. As ever, Toyota rarely went out of its way to publicise developments, but in later years top engineers admitted that one of the problems with the new car was that it was at once too heavy and the as-new-for-rallying shell was too stiff.

Apparently the drivers found that a rally car starting its second or third major event seemed to handle better than it had when it was new, this eventually being proved, scientifically and after much subjective testing, to be due to the way the shells were 'settling' and becoming just a little less stiff in torsion, than when they were new. Private tests with roll cages deliberately made less rigid than originally specified, proved the point, and their layout was accordingly altered.

Early in the season, too, Toyota was disappointed to find that the ST185 was heavier than all its rivals. A snapshot measure came on the organisers' scales in Monte Carlo, where Sainz's car weighed 1206kg, compared with 1149kg for Didier Auriol's Lancia, 1186kg for Francois Delecour's Ford Sierra, and 1178kg for Timo Salonen's Mitsubishi. TTE worked hard at reducing this flab throughout the year. On the Safari, not only did the cars carry specially moulded and shaped fresh air inlet pipes which took their supply from the roof of the car, but they also had massive front end 'roo (for 'kangaroo' – crash protection against animals) bars.

For Corsica, TTE finally unveiled a new-type rear suspension subframe, which was effectively a 'spaceframe' much lighter than the original, and along with other work this made the cars much (up to 40kg, some said) lighter than before. By this time, too, there was water-cooling for the brakes, 17in wheels were used with the latest Pirelli tyres, and cockpit-adjustable anti-roll bars also figured.

During the year, too, the team adopted a Ferguson-type viscous coupling centre-differential in the driveline, which the drivers soon showed was more effective, though it was not until 1993 that this was firmly adopted for all cars, on all events. However, at this stage Toyota could do nothing to counter Lancia's tyre advantage, which meant that the cars could keep going rapidly after a puncture.

For 1993, though, some of these shortcomings were addressed. Not only did Castrol come on board as a major technical (and financial!) sponsor, but Toyota also persuaded Michelin (who had favoured Lancia for some years) to become its tyre supplier (Lancia's official team was being wound-up, though Sainz would continue in a Jolly Club team which inherited many of the Abarth operation's cars, hardware, and some of its technicians), and bring the 'mousse' tyre technology on board.

By this time Dieter Bulling had arrived as TTE's very secretive technical director. At the start of the season, one of his biggest headaches was to optimise the latest Celica GT-Four engine to use the new-fangled 'control' fuel, which was being supplied by Carless. The days of 'rocket fuel,' as supplied to individual teams by their previous sponsors (latterly, in TTE's case, therefore, by Repsol) were over ...

Like all other top teams, too, TTE was experimenting the whole time (sometimes behind the scenes, the results not always being seen on rally cars for ages). Such work eventually included the adoption of oil coolers to control temperatures in the rear differential (nothing new here – Ford had been doing such things with Escorts in the late 1970s!), work on anti-lag engine technology, suspension traction control, along with longer team development of active suspension.

This was the year in which the Catalunya Rally organisers provided a list of World Rally Championship Group A rally car outputs, which rather startled the media. In a formula where the FIA tried to apply a 'nominal' 300bhp, the press release quoted the Celica GT-Four as producing 365bhp, which compared with 355bhp from the Escort RS Cosworth, 385bhp from the Mitsubishi Lancer, and 365bhp from the new Subaru Impreza. Could we believe any of these figures? Maybe so, and maybe not – but Toyota, for sure, was confident that it was no longer running power deficits compared with anyone else.

With the new ST205 Celica already announced, and under rally development, there was no need to bring forward any radical improvements to the old ST185 in 1994, though there seemed to be continuous detail work on engines, on programmable rear hydraulic transmission systems, and in the realms of traction control (which had been pioneered in Finland in 1993). On the Safari, by the way, the team used a viscous central differential for the first time ever in Africa, but this decision was made only after much testing in the run-up to the event.

By mid-1994, the ST185 seemed to have become extremely reliable, and there were few technical novelties still to come, though work continued on the traction control installation. In engineering terms, the end of the 1994 season was rather 'messy,' as the ST185 and new-type ST205 models were used, side-by-side. In fact the new World Champion, Didier Auriol, did not use the ST205 at all in that season, though Juha Kankkunen settled for it after Australia.

According to engineer Dieter Bulling, who concentrated all his efforts on the new car during 1994, the big step forward came with the launch of the ST205 rally car in 1994, which was homologated on 1 May the same year. This was not only a car which looked visually different from the ST185, but one which had many of its own mechanical novelties. Toyota was very cautious about the introduction of this Celica series, sending a Group N car to the 1000 Lakes, and a Group A car to Australia, but the main onslaught would not be until the 1995 season where (as we shall see) the Celica was always a very controversial machine.

The ST205 had several important technical novelties – the aerodynamics (which included the high rear aerofoil section) were claimed to be better, the front suspension was much improved, the wheels on road cars had been increased to 16in (which meant that, under the regulations, 18in Michelins could be used on certain rallies), the structure itself was made more rigid in certain areas, and water-injection was provided for the extremely powerful Group A engine. Not only that, but the 'homologation special' produced by Toyota in 1994 had extra air intakes in the nose, to encourage more and more fresh air to ventilate and feed the well-filled engine bay.

When TTE showed off the Castrol-liveried ST205, in testing, in March 1994, Dieter Bulling made it clear that the 'works' team had been involved with the car right from the start, claiming better aerodynamics, a stiffer basic bodyshell, and water-injection to the turbocharger.

When Toyota was ready to start using the ST205 in World rallies, the company issued this fabulously detailed cut-away drawing of the Group A rally car. Not much space for extra equipment in the engine bay! (Reproduced from the BP/Castrol Archive)

Plus: "Front airflow is much better than on the current car, and the Japanese have followed our requests with regard to positioning of the oil and water radiators ... The wing creates a lot of downforce at the rear without any increase in drag. We haven't had the chance to measure the downforce in rally conditions, but we will go to the wind tunnel later this month."

Before the 1995 season began, the team was obliged to adopt the latest FIA regulations, which reduced the size of turbocharger restrictors from 38mm to 34mm. This hampered the Celica's engine considerably more than the rival engines, it was thought, and we now know that much of Bulling's team efforts during the year were to try to nullify the 'throttling effect' this caused. Early in the year, engine performance was particularly disappointing. Another strategic change was to freeze work on traction control, in favour of electronically-controlled differentials.

Starting in Corsica in the spring, a new type of roll cage assembly was specified, the cars were lightened, and a new type of rear suspension subframe was also adopted. All this work, plus detail improvements to the transmission systems (and a return from Dynamic to Bilstein dampers) was negated when the team was subsequently accused of, and convicted of, cheating over the way that extra air could be channelled around the turbocharger intake to get more into the engine itself.

Once the team had been banned from rallying, Dieter Bulling left the team, most earlier-planned Celica development was halted, and work then concentrated on the new Corolla World Rally Car project. Even so, the team grappled with the outstanding handling deficiencies in 1996 (George Donaldson describes it as having too many moving components in it, with the steering rack not ideally placed, and that: "Some of the drivers used to say that it was like driving a road roller with worm steering ..."), but there was no further work on engine and transmission installations. The suspension change involved a return to MacPherson strut front suspension, and Ohlins dampers were also adopted in place of Bilstein components.

Building and running the 'works' cars

First of all there was Andersson Motorsport, which started life at Uppsala in Sweden, but Toyota Team Europe was then established in Brussels in 1975, before moving to Cologne, Germany, in 1979 when the Toyota operation was still one of the smallest top-level operations in the sport. By the early 1980s, when the rear-drive Celica Twin-Cam Turbo was introduced, TTE had only 17 full-time employees, but a band of up to 25 trusted freelance technicians was already being accumulated. Much larger,

By 1995 the cockpit/fascia/instrument layout of the 'works' cars was very high tech. (Reproduced from the BP/Castrol Archive)

more modern, premises, were then built up, and it was here in Cologne that the four-wheel-drive Toyota Celica GT-Four was unveiled in 1987.

Even in 1988, in the Acropolis Rally, in the Celica's first year at World level, team boss Ove Andersson stressed that Toyota had a lot to learn:

"We must be realistic, as this is only our second event with four-wheel-drive. Lancia have been working with 4WD and that car [the Delta Integrale] for a long time, they are still the people setting the standard – I think that they have about 200 employees at Abarth.

This is certainly a time of growth for Toyota Team Europe, we have 66 people, plus others who are brought in for events … what happened with the loss of Henry Liddon [the much-respected co-ordinator who had been killed in Africa when a service/supervision plane had crashed] meant that it will take a long time to rebuild. Henry left an enormous hole, he was like a father to all of us."

For the next three years or so, Jurgen Bertl (ex-Audi) became Ove's co-ordinator, but by the early 1990s it was Maurice Guaslard (ex-Michelin, French, and something of a tyre expert) who held the position of Team Manager, though Ove was ever-present on all events which TTE tackled. Phil Short (who is profiled below) then arrived in 1992, and became TTE's official Team Manager until the end of 1994, though to do this job he had to live in Germany, and see little of his wife and family.

When Phil returned to the UK, George Donaldson (who was one of the team's co-ordinators) was promoted, and managed the team for Ove until the end (and beyond) of the Celica project. He finally left Toyota in 2000, when rallying activity ended, and Formula One took over instead.

Subsequently, he performed similar duties with Subaru/Prodrive in the UK.

Phil, as generous as ever in his praise for unsung members of the team, reminded me that Dagobert Rohrer was a valuable engineer who concentrated on African and other endurance events, and that Gerhard Pfeiffer (most colleagues knew him as Gert Pepper) was the principal testing and on-event engineer in other non-African events. Solve Andreasson of Sweden (who had been another successful co-driver in the 1970s), also provided much managerial, behind the scenes, back up.

Although the team's man-power got larger and larger as the programme, and the budget (aided by sponsors like Castrol and Marlboro) increased, Ove Andersson was never just a figurehead. After his untimely death in 2008, he was described by no less an obituarist than Martin Brundle, as a man with a 'velvet glove concealing an iron fist,' and several personalities have pointed out that he always seemed to know *everything* that was going on in this very professional operation.

At any one time, the fleet of 'works' cars at Cologne was rather smaller than it sometimes seemed, this being because of the rather profligate way in which vehicle identities were used on events. Although I have listed each and every one of the identities seen on TTE-owned/TTE-controlled Celicas (see page 120), the fact is that some cars used different numbers on different rallies. This was apparently a particular German process, connected with the insurance of a particular machine at a particular time.

[Ideally, this book should of course post a list of TTE's internal 'TC' numbers – which would show that rather fewer cars than the registration numbers indicate, were actually

Who owned who?

In the beginning, the 'works' Toyota GT-Fours were prepared and run by Toyota Team Europa, the company running that organisation being Andersson Motorsport. From mid-1993, however, the Toyota parent company in Japan exercised its buy-out rights by forming Toyota Motorsport GmbH, a new company whose president was still Ove Andersson, and which initially employed 220 people. The change, it transpired, was mainly legal and administrative, and seemed to make no difference to the running of the rally team.

Hot, dusty, and under pressure at a service point, with George Donaldson (centre, with headband) assessing the problem. (Courtesy Phil Short)

built – but because some authoritative Toyota historians do not want to see falsely-registered cars with so-called 'famous' histories re-created, I have not been provided with this list].

As to the staff and personnel, the numbers grew and grew until the FIA began to apply a 'cap' in 1994 and 1995. Even on a relatively compact European event, if conditions were demanding, it was likely that up to 150 people would be supporting three rally cars, and that there would be at least fifteen to eighteen full service vans, along with a fleet of chase cars, management cars, one or more helicopters and two or more catering motor-homes. At any one time, up to twenty different nationalities would be represented!

Phil Short, who had to administer the on-event operations for years, told me that Lancia was still the largest team until about 1992, but by the time the Celica was at its peak in 1993 and 1994, Toyota was employing even more people, and enjoying even more resources:

"On the Acropolis, for instance, there were certain stages where, if you sent in a service vehicle the day before, to a certain village, he would then drive over a certain stage, position himself between the two of which might be critical stages for the following day – and they would be stuck there until the rally had passed, and the roads had been opened up again. This gave us an advantage over rivals who were not able to place a service vehicle there ..."

Neat, tidy, full-equipped, and as meticulously organised as every other aspect of TTE, this is one of TTE's 'works' service vans. (Courtesy Phil Short)

Disqualification, and the leaking turbo affair of 1995

The history of this Toyota rally car project would be incomplete without an analysis of the 'turbo affair' of 1995 – where the 'works' Celicas were found to be using illegally-modified turbochargers in the Catalunya Rally in October, after which the team was unceremoniously pitched out of the World Championship, losing all its points for the entire season, and being banned from competition for the whole of 1996. As a dedicated rally historian, I would be naïve if I tried to ignore the events surrounding it, and the personalities involved.

There is no doubt that the engine specification used in Catalunya was totally illegal – as will be explained, this involved using turbochargers which passed extra air, other than that which passed through the compulsory 34mm diameter restrictor. The crisis that engulfed TTE on the 1995 Catalunya Rally had its roots in an earlier World Rally – which was the Australian event, where quite phenomenal acceleration seemed to be available from standing starts, and up steep inclines. However, on reflection, and after a study of stage times, there was evidence that the cheating had begun earlier than that.

When observed on the 'Superspecial' stage, which was mounted in Langley

Dieter Bulling became TTE's top engineer in the early 1990s, and was mainly responsible for late-model ST185 and all the ST205 developments.

Park, Perth, on the Rally Australia, it was clear that in the initial 300-metre tarmac 'drag race' off the start line, the Toyotas were appreciably quicker than any other car in the event. On the basis that all cars had to run with the same turbo-restricted 2-litre engines, and all had four-wheel-drive, this was difficult to accept, or to understand.

When the Celicas were seen to be so very fast on the next event – Catalunya 1995 – and that Juha Kankkunen, not a tarmac specialist, was comfortably leading the tarmac event over the first 15 special stages, suspicions deepened. Uncorroborated stories report that a disgruntled, ex-TTE employee had acted as a whistle-blower to alert officials, but the fact is FIA technical delegate Jacques Berger suddenly demanded a supply of spare, sealed, turbochargers from each of the factory teams in the event – Toyota, Mitsubishi, Subaru and Ford – and took them away for detailed examination.

The result was that the TTE turbocharger was seen to have been ingeniously, and quite illegally, modified so that: (1) the restrictor was not sealed, so it was possible to move it without touching the [FIA scrutineers'] seals; (2) it was possible for additional air to enter the engine without passing the restrictor and; (3) the position of the restrictor could be moved so that it was further away from the [turbo] turbine than the 50mm limit permitted by regulations.

Simply, World rallying rules had been written so as to impose the same 34mm diameter restrictor upstream of the turbocharger of every Group A car, this automatically imposing an approximate 300bhp peak output on every engine. On the latest engine from TTE, however, ways had been found of getting more air into the engine than this, and since more air equals more power, the result was obvious.

When the FIA handed down its judgement, which was naturally accepted by TTE because they had been caught red-handed, President Max Mosley commented that the modified air inlet system was: "… the most sophisticated and ingenious device I have ever seen in 30 years of motorsport, or indeed had any other member of the World Council, scrutineers or technical experts. The marvel of the system was that it

By the time the ST205 became Toyota's front line rally car, the engine bay of this turbocharged 2-litre car was as full as possible. Cooling was always a challenge – usually conquered.

The drive that unleashed the whirlwind came in Spain/Calalunya in 1995, where Juha Kankkunen, of all people, put in a stunning tarmac drive to outpace everyone. This, to say the least, was inexplicable, and resulted in the team's turbocharger installation being denounced as illegal, and the team banned from World Rallying for the whole of 1996.

was completely concealed under a hose which encased the restrictor and joined the turbocharger with the air filter. When the system was dismantled there was no way of telling anything irregular had existed."

Mosley said the system was put into operation when the restrictor was assembled. As the restrictor was attached to the turbocharger body, it was covered by an all-encasing hose. This hose was then tightened with three jubilee clips. One of these required a special tool to operate it, because *it was used to pull the restrictor outwards from its casing*. This movement not only served to aid the airflow into the turbine blades, but more importantly opened up a 5mm gap through which extra air could enter the engine on the engine side of the legal constriction.

All in all, this was demonstrably a device that had taken months to design and develop, and it was clear that

TTE never intended any other team or individual (nor, it seems, the drivers or many of the managers) to know of the stratagem.

Because the author is not entirely clear as to the responsibility for the development of this device, names cannot be named. However, it can be said that Ove Andersson readily accepted responsibility for everything that went on within his company, that certain engineering and development personnel left the company soon after the debacle was exposed, and that Ove not only survived the farrago, but was able to get approval from Toyota for the next-generation rally car, the Corolla WRC, to be developed.

The Corolla WRC, in fact, would use modified versions of the ST205's engine and X-Trac four-wheel-drive transmission but not, repeat not, anything tricky in the turbocharger restrictor department.

Personalities and star drivers
Ove Andersson

Although Swedish-born Ove Anderson ran a Toyota team that was accused of sharp practice on several occasions, and sometimes convicted, none of the resulting shame which caused the Japanese marque to suffer a loss of face ever seemed to rub off on him. The fact that he *must* have known of the events which sometimes exploded in the team's face, never caused anyone to turn against him, which was something of a miracle.

From the mid-1970s, when he set up Toyota Team Europe, to 2003, when he finally retired from business, he was the head of the European Toyota motorsport operation, universally liked and respected by almost everyone who knew him.

Originally a garage mechanic in Sweden, he soon took up rallying, joined the Saab, Lancia, Ford, Renault and Peugeot rally teams, and won several World events, including the Monte Carlo and Safari rallies, before settling for Toyota (first as a driver, then as the team boss) when cars were simple and pressures were few. Surprisingly, Toyota chose to settle its team in Germany, rather than in Andersson's native Sweden, which may have been technically wise in the long run.

Ove Andersson set up TTE in the 1970s, and guided the Celica GT-Four through its successful decade of front line rallying.

Although Toyota was left behind by the technological avalanche that accompanied Group B in the 1980s (when the elephantine Celica Twin-Cam Turbo was launched, Ove candidly told the press: "I asked for four-wheel-drive – but I got *this* …"), ground was rapidly made up in the Celica GT-Four era, and with the Corolla WRCs that followed.

The quietly spoken, but infinitely experienced Andersson unerringly picked a number of excellent associates – Henry Liddon, Phil Short and George Donaldson all being successful Team Managers – and built up a remarkable record of success and, it has to be said, controversy at the Cologne HQ. Even a health scare – he needed a heart bybass operation in 1994 to restore him to full vigour – did not deter him. Indeed, when using the Corolla WRC, the rally team was still at its height at the end of the 1990s when Toyota (not Ove Andersson) elected to abandon the sport, and to enter Formula One racing instead (where, if the truth be told, it failed to make much impact for ten entire seasons).

Having retired at the end of 2003 (he was already 65 years of age), Ove then took up other interests, but never completely lost contact with rallying. Tragically, it was when enjoying himself by competing in a classic event in South Africa that he was killed in a road crash.

TTE was usually too busy to pose for team portraits, but here Ove Andersson made an exception. Ove himself takes centre stage while behind him (left to right) are Peter Diekmann, Kenneth Eriksson, Juha Piironen, Björn Waldegård, I Bertl and Juha Kankkunen.

Before he founded TTE, Ove Andersson (right) was a successful rally driver. Here he is with Bill Meade of Ford Motorsport.

Henry Liddon

Although Bristol-born Henry Liddon was killed in a private plane crash before the Celica GT-Four even made its debut, he was a vitally important part of the TTE operation from 1980 to 1987. Already legendary in the world of rallying, where he had been a winning co-driver at World level with drivers such as Timo Makinen, and Ove Andersson at Ford, Peugeot, and Toyota, he became TTE's team co-ordinator in 1980, and helped build up that organisation in the years which followed.

As an organiser, he was involved in the World Cup Rally (London-Kano-Munich) of 1974, and dabbled in motoring journalism later in the 1970s, but concentrated on co-ordination after that. It was Henry's calm, unflappable, courteous and always kindly manner which helped Toyota win several African and Asian classics during the 1980s, and, when Ove Andersson set about the evolution of the new Celica GT-Four, Henry was one of his closest confidants.

Tragically, it was on the Ivory Coast Rally of September 1987 that Henry, along with Nigel Harris and the pilot of the light plane being used for communications purposes,

Although tragically killed in a plane crash before the Celica GT-Four made its debut in 1988, Henry Liddon was Ove Andersson's No 2, Team Manager, guru and confidante in the formative years.

was killed instantly when the Cessna crashed on take off. TTE's Supra Turbos, need it be said, were dominating the event at the time, and it was typical of Ove Andersson that he immediately withdrew all of them to see if anything could be done for Henry. It could not, and everyone in rallying was shattered. He was only 55 years old.

Phil Short

Yorkshire-born Phil Short got into rallying as a hobby, soon becoming a noted co-driver (among others, with Ford's John Taylor), before getting together with David Llewellin, originally to drive Audi Quattros in the British Championship.

After Audi withdrew from rallying, David and Phil moved to a Toyota-GB-run Toyota Celica GT-Four programme, in which they quite dominated the British Championship in 1989 and 1990. During the 1970s and 1980s, and while Henry Liddon was TTE's team manager, TTE began hiring vans from Phil's Bradford-based hire concern, which was where the original links were forged.

Phil Short was already a successful co-driver before he teamed up with David Llewellin to win British events in Celica GT-Fours. In the 1990s he moved to Cologne, to become a service co-ordinator, and later team manager of TTE.

Later, and after Henry was tragically killed in a plane crash in the Ivory Coast, team manager Maurice Guaslard began using Phil as an 'ice notes' and 'weather' crew member, and within months he was also asked to co-ordinate a Belgian/European programme for Patrick Snyers' Belgian team, running a well-prepared GT-Four, which originated from Reinhard Hainbach of Germany.

From this point, it was just a short jump for Phil to become Ove Andersson's World Championship team co-ordinator, based at Cologne. Phil recalls that TTE had such a multi-national group of staff in those days that even though the team was in Germany, the 'usual language' spoken was English!

Phil then took over the team manager's job from Maurice Guaslard in early-1992 (Jurgen Bertl worked for him for a time), on a three-year contract, which he duly honoured, until he left at the end of 1994 to join Ralliart (of Rugby, GB), which was running the Mitsubishi cars. It was during this period that he encouraged George Donaldson to become a team co-ordinator rather than a workshop manager, so when the time came for him to leave the transition was both logical, and immediate.

In more recent years. Phil went on to become the strategic 'eyes and ears' of the 'works' Ford/M-Sport rally team.

George Donaldson

Scottish-born Donaldson gained rally inspiration by watching the RAC Rally in the 1970s, then by competing as a private owner. Earning a crust as a mechanic, he then got to know organisers like Fred Gallagher and Henry Liddon, started learning the profession of rally co-ordination, then became a freelance mechanic (a 'mercenary,' as they were affectionately known in the sport) for Toyota in 1985, and was connected with the team until 2000. Widely-separated weeks of work, not only as a rally mechanic, but as a hard-working 'mud-crew' driver and general dogsbody, then led to him working more and more intensely for Henry Liddon at Toyota in the days when TTE was running Celica Twin-Cam Turbos, and normally-aspirated Supras.

Although George won the Ford Rallysearch

George Donaldson began his TTE career as a jobbing mechanic, rose through the ranks to become a co-ordinator in the early 1990s, and then Team Manager in 1995.

competition in 1987, and subsequently ran a Group N Sierra RS Cosworth (a programme that included winning the Group N category in the RAC Rally), he packed in his active driving career at the end of 1988, and became a full-time technician/mechanic and – soon – workshop organiser for Toyota.

From mid-1989, he spent much time in Kenya, where TTE had a virtually permanent test and development workshop for the Safari cars, and became Workshop Manager. By the time Phil Short became Team Manager, George became a full-time Co-ordinator. By 1993 he was Short's trusted right-hand-man. As Phil Short has already told the author, when he (Short) decided to return to the UK, George Donaldson was the obvious, and most suitable, personality to take over from him, which he did in the second half of the 1990s.

George, therefore, was TTE's leading co-ordinator during the Celica's 'golden' period – 1993 and 1994 – and Team Manager from 1995 onwards, when controversy seemed to surround the ST205 cars.

Carlos Sainz

No-one ever had a bad word to say about Carlos, the multi-talented Spaniard who was well connected in Spanish court circles, and could equally have made a successful professional sporting career in football, squash or tennis. First 'discovered' by Ford in 1987, he moved on to Toyota in 1989, then to Lancia and Subaru before re-joining Ford for 1996 and 1997. Along the way, he won the World Drivers' Championship twice, always gave his all to the team that was employing him, and in two separate stints with Toyota – 1989-1992 and 1998-1999 – he recorded fifteen outright victories, along with an astonishing seventeen second and ten third places. Thirteen of those outright wins were in four-wheel-drive Celicas. Almost single-handedly, it seemed, he established the Celica's reputation as a winning car in 1989, bringing self-belief and faith in the cars back to a team that had previously been struggling with obsolete two-wheel-drive machines.

Not only supreme and very consistent on tarmac, loose surfaces, or ice and snow, Carlos was one of the best and most dedicated test drivers in the business. Cultured, polite and helpful to everyone he ever met, he was liked by every one, loved by most of the Spanish nation, and an inspiration to any rally team. It was no wonder that Ove Andersson spent several persistent weeks wooing him towards the end of 1988, although he had to spend much time convincing his Japanese masters that such an expensive signing was necessary to the brand's rallying future.

Although he and Ove Andersson had a warm personal relationship, before the end of 1992 it was a clash of existing and potential oil company sponsors that caused Carlos to leave TTE. With Castrol just about to arrive at TTE as major headline sponsor, Sainz's oil company supporter from Spain, Repsol, was sidelined – so the much-respected Spaniard was therefore obliged to walk away.

Having left Toyota after 1992, he would certainly have returned earlier than he did to drive the final Celicas, but because the team was banned from the sport in 1996, for technical infringements in 1995, there was suddenly no programme for him to tackle and he joined Ford instead, though he eventually came back to Toyota to drive the Corolla World Rally Cars.

World Champion of 1990 and 1992, Carlos Sainz, in deep discussion with team-mates and Pirelli technicians. No detail was ever too insignificant for Carlos to ignore! (Courtesy Phil Short)

If ever a car prospered by the efforts and talents of one man, it was the Celica – and Carlos Sainz. Twice World Champion in Toyotas, Carlos was an inspiration to all who knew him.

was their attitude to testing. Armin Schwarz would test for weeks, Carlos would test for months, but Juha would only test for hours."

Juha Kankkunen

Although he started rallying in Finland in 1978, in his own Escort RS2000, Juha Kankkunen did not originally join Toyota's 'works' team until mid-1983, his first victories coming (in Celica Twin-Cam Turbos) in 1985. In a long career he then drove Peugeots, Lancias, Toyotas (again) Lancias (again) and Toyotas (again), before finding himself out of work in 1996 after Toyota was thrown out of World rallying for cheating over engine/turbocharger restrictor

Juha Kankkunen won the World Drivers' Championship four times – using ST185s to win for Toyota in 1993.

By the time he retired from the sport in 2004, having spent yet more time with Ford, then one unhappy season with Citroën, he had won no fewer than 26 World rallies.

As George Donaldson told me about Carlos:

"If you sat in a car with Carlos, he was much more aggressive than Juha. He never seemed to coax a car, he forced a car to do everything. He might not have been the most natural driver, but I will always insist that he is the greatest driver of our time. He liked a very reactive car that maximised its traction. The difference between them all infringements. His final 'works' appearances then came with Subaru at the end of the 1990s.

Although not known as one of rallying's deep thinkers or communicators, he was a naturally talented driver, a true natural, who seemed to be happier on loose surfaces or a golf course, than on tarmac and in press conferences. He was, nevertheless, consistently fast, very rarely crashed his cars, and was a great team man (which he had to be, on occasion, when he had to give way to Carlos Sainz. If one was being brutally honest, Juha always gave the impression of driving as little as possible, testing as little as possible, and enjoying himself outside the car as much as possible. He was, on the other hand, often content to drive a less than perfect car, and produced great results with some faltering machinery.

His dislike of testing (or, should one say, his low boredom threshold) was well-known:

"Juha would come along after everyone else had finished testing," Donaldson recalls, "The first thing he would do would be take a whole lot of poundage out of the springs, soften the car right off, lower it quite a bit, find the optimum balance, and that was it – two hours! Although the other drivers might be sure their settings were better, they would drive Juha's settings. Juha would be faster in the early stages of events, and they would then change to his settings …"

All in all, he became World Rally Champion no fewer than four times in the 1980s and 1990s – Toyota provided the cars in 1993 – and recorded 23 individual World Rally victories. In nine widely-separated seasons with Toyota, he won nine World rallies, taking seven second places, and eight thirds.

Didier Auriol

Like Carlos and Juha, Didier Auriol of France drove for several teams in a World rallying career spanning seventeen years. His first World victory was for Ford, in Corsica, in 1988, but although he only won the World Championship once, with Toyota in 1994, he won nineteen World events. He drove for the Toyota team from 1993 to 1995, then from 1997 to 1999. In his World Championship-winning year he notched up three outright victories.

In every way the archetypal mercurial Frenchman – team personalities described him as a very intense character, riddled with character traits, sometime nervy and rarely seeming to be relaxed in the rally environment. It was sometimes said of Didier that, for him to succeed, the car needed to be absolutely perfect – but if it wasn't, then he really couldn't drive around the problem.

Auriol seemed to be followed around by controversy over regulations and their interpretation. Several puzzling discrepancies occurred with the Lancias during Auriol's time with the team (mention nitrous-oxide fuel additives to any Italian engineer, and they will immediately mention Lancia …), while at Toyota, he was suspected of driving a car that was drinking illegal substances, then was a team member when the cars were banned from motorsport because of turbocharger infringements – but Auriol was a ruthless go-getter who only wanted to win, and not just to be known as a 'good chap.'

He did not join TTE until 1993, effectively as a direct swap for Carlos Sainz, as Auriol left Lancia for Toyota at the end of the 1992 season, just as Sainz was on his way out of the door. Rumours and counter-romours had been spreading about the two of them ending up in the same team for 1993, but on a personal basis this rarely looked likely, as there was too much professional animosity between them.

It took Auriol some time to settle at Toyota – he had, after all, been driving for Lancia for the previous four seasons, so (as Phil Short reminded me: "There was quite a bit of 'Lancia used to do it this way …' in his early dealings with us"), but he settled well in 1994, and won the World Drivers' Championship in that season. It was unfortunate that he then found himself driving for the team when it was found to be cheating over turbocharger regularities, which meant that he was released for 1996. He later returned to drive the Corolla World Rally Car.

Opposite page: The newly-crowned World Rally Champion, Didier Auriol, was expecting great things of the ST205 in 1995. Unhappily, the latest car was hampered by the new 34mm diameter turbo restrictor rule, and Auriol later crashed it. (Reproduced from the BP/Castrol Archive)

Competition story

The 'works' Celica GT-Four's career
As already noted, once Group B (and its off-shoot, Group S) was abruptly cancelled in mid-1986, it meant that TTE had to scrap all existing programmes and start again. Not even the hard-working TT team (and their pay masters in Japan) could achieve a miracle in ultra-quick time, so the original 'works' Celica GT-Four was not homologated in Group A until 1 May 1988.

TTE, of course, was well-prepared for this date, and had been testing assiduously before then. Just two days after the new car had achieved Group A status, two cars made their debut in Corsica. On that weekend, Kenneth Eriksson took sixth place: four months later Juha Kankkunen's car led the 1000 Lakes Rally for many miles, and the first podium finish came in the British RAC Rally at the end of that year. Thereafter, the four-wheel-drive Toyotas were always potential victors, and remained so for almost a decade.

1988
The season had started modestly for Toyota, with no 'works' entries in Monte Carlo, Sweden or Portugal. The team then returned on the Safari, with three front-engine/rear-drive Supra Turbos, and the star-studded driver line-up of Juha Kankkunen, Björn Waldegård and Kenneth Eriksson. These cars finished strongly – in fifth, sixth and eighth places – emphasising that the team, at least, had lost nothing in the way of experience, preparation skills and rally know-how.

Immediately after homologation had been achieved, two Celica GT-Fours (of ST165-type, carrying registration/identity numbers K-AM2130 and K-AM3787, though as I explain at the back of the book, these were not always significant) then appeared on the Tour de Corse, an event dominated by the titanic battle between the Lancia Integrales and Didier Auriol's 'works' Ford Sierra RS Cosworth. Although the Toyotas were never on the pace,

Peter Diekmann was Kenneth Eriksson's co-driver in the TTE team.

Kenneth Eriksson, from Sweden, was one of TTE's contracted drivers at the start of the Celica GT-Four programme.

Björn Waldegård became World Rally Champion in 1979, the first season in which this contest was promoted. In the 1980s he crowned his career with Toyota, winning several events for TTE in Africa.

they impressed everyone with their poise, and with their generally high-level of preparation.

Even though the team had already completed 5000 miles (8000km) of testing in Corsica, the cars were not nearly as specialised as they would become. As Ove Andersson quoted before the start: "We are warming up to our new, bigger, team. This is just the beginning, and this is the reason for us to be at the rally." Even so, the cars looked good, and made a good impression. It was really no surprise that Kankkunen's car broke its engine, for the good news was that Eriksson's car finished a solid sixth place.

The Acropolis, which followed just weeks later, was a different challenge – rough where the Tour de Corse had been smooth, dusty where the Tour de Corse had been clear, and requiring new, different and physically stronger cars. This time there were just two new cars (K-AM2051 and K-AM6782), driven by Kankkunen and Waldegård but neither made it to the finish. After only two stages, Waldegård's car broke its Xtrac transmission, and soon after half-distance Kankkunen's car retired, not only due to repeated problems with the transmission, but with engine failure.

The 'works' Celica GT-Four made its first appearance in the Tour de Corse of May 1988, where the car was seen looking very smart, but still under powered – a failing which would soon be rectified. Left-to-right: Juha Piironen, Juha Kankkunen and Kenneth Eriksson.

Juha Kankkunen in the Acropolis Rally of 1988, where the rough, tough and dusty conditions gave the new GT-Fours a hard time. As can be seen from the livery, Pirelli (tyres) and Duckhams (oils/lubricants) were important trade sponsors.

That was the bad news. The great news was that, even with engines which still needed much more power (and it was promised, though not for some months) the cars were already competitive. On the Acropolis, Kankkunen led the entire event briefly, and set six fastest stage times – which worried the opposition, particularly Lancia, considerably.

Toyota then missed several events, concentrating on getting more cars, and the still-evolving team, ready for the 1000 Lakes in Finland, where Kankkunen and Eriksson were both, as it were, on home ground. Though both cars eventually retired – one with broken transmission, the other with engine failure – they did not disappoint. Kankkunen set no fewer than seventeen fastest stage times (there were 39 stages, all in all) and was leading the entire event when he was forced to drop out. Xtrac transmission woes were still evident, which caused Eriksson to retire, but it was a sudden engine failure (thought to be related to valve gear) which stopped Kankkunen on Stage 34. Then, as later, Toyota was secretive about its failures – for the Japanese did not like 'losing face' and did not like to admit to shortcomings.

Toyota, to be frank, needed a victory to boost its morale, and fortunately one soon followed – in the Cyprus Rally of September, this being a second-level European, rather than a World Championship, round. TTE, though, took it very seriously, as the stages were hot, rough and demanding – which was ideal 'development' territory. Both cars, driven by Björn Waldegård and Kenneth Eriksson, headed up every other car in the event, and though Eriksson was eventually forced out when a puncture led to a lost road wheel. Waldegård, however, the 'old master,' eased home his Celica, Xtrac problems not withstanding, and finally won by nearly eight minutes from Fabrizio Tabaton's Lancia.

Even so, it was brave of the team to enter two more new cars for the five-day San Remo event in October, if only because this was really Lancia's 'home event.' Unhappily, the Lancias proved to be altogether too fast – and reliable – for the Toyotas. Not only was Lancia *the* dominant marque in World rallying at the time, but this particular event might have been designed (maybe it *was* so designed) to suit the Deltas. Ford, for example, led the first two days, on tarmac, in its rear-drive Sierra RS Cosworths, but slumped when the event turned to loose surfaces. Toyota, for its part, still lacked the sheer power, and the agile handling, that was needed so emphatically in Italy on this event. Although Kenneth Eriksson's Celica set seven fastest stage times (and nine second and third fastests) this was not enough: when Kankkunen put his Celica off the road, backwards and irrevocably, sixth place for Eriksson was all which could be achieved in the end.

Five weeks later, three Celicas were entered for the British RAC Rally, where almost all the stages were on gravel surfaces, and that much-coveted victory was so nearly achieved. But it was not to be – and although Kankkunen battled for the lead until the last day, setting 13 fastest special stage times, it was Markku Alen's Lancia Delta Integrale that was consistently faster. Kenneth Eriksson's rally lasted for just 300 yards into the first stage before the engine cam belt broke – and that was that. Björn Waldegård was there and thereabouts for five days – he was fourth at half distance, and third overall at the finish, but plagued by punctures – although it was the unfortunate Kankkunen who made the headlines.

Still in the lead as the final day's run – Harrogate to the Yorkshire stages, then back to Harrogate – began, Juha eventually made a mistake:

"We were within sight of the end of Stage 44, with only seven more stages left, when I went off a little and hit a tree. This broke the oil cooler ... As soon as we got going again the oil pressure failed, and we were out of the event ..."

Because of the paucity of ex-works cars, and a general shortage of dedicated parts, it took time for the Celica GT-Four to become a winner at European Championship level. Indeed, without Björn Waldegård's second place in the German Hunsruck (August) and victory, as already mentioned, in Cyprus, there would have been nothing to boast about. In Britain, too, there were no competitive Celicas, though at the end of the year came the exciting news that for 1989 David Llewellin would have a full programme in a privately prepared car.

Björn Waldegård gave the GT-Four its first 'podium' finish at the end of 1988, by taking third place on the RAC Rally.

Sometimes it would have been better to stay in bed! Björn Waldegård's Celica suffered a puncture in mid-stage of the 1988 RAC Rally and a wheel had to be changed. Waldegård (already back in the car) and Fred Gallagher have just finished the job, which dropped them a place – from second overall to third.

Phil Collins' preparation company got the job of building Celica GT-Fours for David Llewellin to use in the British Championship, which he duly won in 1989 and 1990.

1989

For 1989, the big change was that Carlos Sainz joined the team, having spent two frustrating years in rear-wheel-drive Ford Sierra RS Cosworths. The ever-gentlemanly Spaniard had not wanted to let Ford down (they had, after all, picked him out of obscurity in 1986), but once it became clear that there would be no competitive four-wheel-drive Sierra until 1990, he forged bonds with Toyota, and soon established a lasting friendship with Ove Andersson and all the staff.

Andersson, therefore, had a formidable driving team for 1989 – Eriksson, Kankkunen, and Waldegård were all retained too – but still found that it was still going to take ages for the first World victory to follow – which would be in Australia, towards the end of the year. Not even the remarkably ambitious, and dedicated, Sainz, could speed up that process. Several important events – New Zealand, for instance – were not even in the programme.

How long would it be, in 1989, before new team recruit Carlos Sainz could start winning in the ST165?

Kenneth Eriksson of Sweden was one of TTE's front line drivers in the early days of the Celica GT-Four project.

Duncan fifth), two further-developed tarmac-specification 'works' Celicas then took the start in the Tour de Corse, along with a near-identical 'Bastos' car for Patrick Snyers. Although they could not quite keep up with the all-conquering Lancias (Didier Auriol was in scintillating form), and Juha Kankkunen never hid his distaste for tarmac rallying, they were nonetheless competitive, setting a handful of fastest stage times.

Although two cars retired with what might be described as 'typical' Celica failures – broken transmission in Snyers's car, and a blown engine in Sainz's machine – Kankkunen kept going, eventually to finish third, nearly four minutes behind the victorious Lancia. But the gap was closing, Toyota's experience was continuing to build – and the first victory was surely not to be long delayed?

In Monte Carlo, the Celicas were still significantly slower than the all-conquering Lancias, though Sainz soon showed he had rapidly come to terms with the new car and team, by setting faster times than Kankkunen. Unhappily, Sainz then made a wrong choice of tyres on an icy stage and went off the road, Waldegård's car suffered engine failure, and Kankkunen could only finish fifth, 15 minutes behind Miki Biasion's winning Lancia.

Not only was there a repeat performance in Portugal in March – with Lancia finishing 1-2-3 – but all three of the 'works' Celicas failed to finish, and only Sainz set a handful of fastest stage times before having to abandon. Sainz crashed out after 15 stages, Kankkunen's engine let go just two stages later, and Waldegård's transmission broke on the start-line of a stage soon afterwards when he was the only non-Lancia vying for the lead.

Having sent two old-style Supra Turbos to compete in the Safari (where Waldegård took fourth place, and Ian

It did not follow, however, on the Acropolis, in Greece, where all four of the official cars dropped out of the event. The fact that Juha Kankkunen's car set the most fastest stage times – 12 fastest times out of the 42 stages – was no consolation for an event where Eriksson's car suffered a fire following leaking hydraulic fluid, Snyers' car broke its engine, while both Sainz and Kankkunen eventually retired with the front suspension, and bodyshells around them, breaking up under the strain.

After a summer lay-off, TTE then entered the A-team of three Celicas for the Finnish 1000 Lakes, where both Kankkunen, then Sainz, led the entire rally until about half distance. Unhappily, Kankkunen's car then suffered an engine fire (cause not clear) that destroyed the engine bay, and when Carlos was battling for the lead, he rolled his brand-new car on Stage 27, losing four minutes and two places. Although he set many fastest stage times, he could only take third place, two-and-a-half minutes off the pace.

All the drama of a Monte Carlo Rally service point in 1989, with Juha Kankkunen's ST165 receiving attention. (Courtesy Phil Short)

By 1989, the ST165 was still looking for its first success at the start of the season. Juha Kankkunen took fifth in Monte Carlo.

By mid-1989 the Celica GT-Four was almost ready to begin winning. This was Juha Kankkunen on his way to third place in Corsica.

Australia, though, was a different story. Two new cars were shipped all the way from Germany, to be driven by Kankkunen and Eriksson. Naturally, there was a stage-by-stage battle against the Lancia Deltas, but on this occasion the Toyotas were always dominant. The result – long overdue as far as TTE, its drivers, and its growing fanbase were concerned – was that Juha won the event, by just 67 seconds, from team-mate Eriksson. Between them, the Toyotas set 29 fastest stage times (of 32 stages in all), and the team never really looked like being beaten. Quite suddenly, Lancia began to look vulnerable – and the Toyota began to look like a potential World Champion.

The fight-back came at once. In Italy, in San Remo, Lancia not only used the newly-homologated 16-valve Integrale for the first time, but won with it also. Though Carlos Sainz battled for the lead until the very last minute, at only four stages from the end, his car suddenly suffered a jammed throttle linkage, and he faltered. In the end, he finished third, just 25 seconds behind the winning Lancia.

As ever, it was the British RAC Rally which provided the climax to the season; the prospect of a three-way battle between Toyota, Lancia and Mitsubishi. Lancia withdrew a few days before the start (citing the need for more pre-1990 testing, but widely thought to be because it had already secured World Championships, and was not looking forward to being beaten in Britain …). In five days of pulsating competition, there were no fewer than 55 special stages.

A great occasion for Toyota! Juha Kankkunen drove K-AM5108 to outright victory in Rally Australia in September 1989. There would be many more wins to follow this one …

F70 LPH was the first of three ST165s used by David Llewellin to dominate the British Rally Championship in 1989 and 1990. Here he was on the car's second event in 1989, the Circuit of Ireland, where mechanical problems forced him out.

Five different drivers led from time to time – and in the end it was only mechanical disaster which robbed Sainz of a much deserved victory.

Juha Kankkunen led at first, Erikkson then took over, but from Stage 16 it seemed to be a straight Sainz-Kankkunen battle. Until the last morning, that is, in the fast and smooth stages of North Yorkshire when a quite unexpected challenge from Pentti Airikkala's Mitsubishi Galant VR4 became serious. Suddenly, with only three stages to complete, the propeller shaft of Carlos's Celica suddenly snapped, leaving the car with only front-wheel-drive in the very long Dalby stage. At a stroke, Carlos lost 126 seconds to the Mitsubishi – and that was that. From leading – and leading with real

Welshman David Llewellin dominated the British rally scene in 1989 and 1990, driving Celica GT-Fours prepared by Phil Collins in workshops close to Hereford.

merit – Carlos suddenly had to settle for second place, his team-mate Kankkunen following him home in third place. It was no way to end what had been such as promising season.

Victories, on the other hand, finally began to mount up at European Championship level, starting with Patrick Snyers' Bastos-backed win in the Boucles de Spa in February, though the next did not follow until Kenneth Eriksson won in South Sweden in May. Carlos Sainz also won at this level, too, using one of Ove Andersson's cars. It was already clear that the ubiquitous Lancia Delta Integrale was facing really tough opposition.

In the British Rally Championship, the formidable combination of Celica GT-Four (prepared by Phil Collins), David Llewellin (driver) and Phil Short (co-driver/team-manager), dominated the season in two different cars – F70 LPH and F88 LPH. Not only did this combination win four of the seven events in the series (all the gravel-surface stage events), but they were competitive on tarmac, too, taking third behind two Sierra RS Cosworths.

David Llewellin's cars dominated British motorsport in 1989 and 1990. This car, his second (of three), is on its way to briefly leading the 1989 RAC Rally, before it broke a driveshaft and had to retire.

1990

The big change in 1990 was that Juha Kankkunen had torn up his Toyota contract to move back to Lancia, and would no longer be in a Celica. It was not that he thought the Lancia to be a better car – the evidence was that Toyota was its equal, as Carlos Sainz was about to prove – but that in 1989 he had been frustrated by a series of mechanical breakdowns which had robbed him of more than one success. This, though, was not the end of his relationship with Toyota – he would be back!

It is also worth noting that although the existing Celica GT-Four had already been rendered obsolete in the showrooms (the new – ST185 – model had been launched at the Tokyo Motor Show at the end of 1989), TTE made it clear that it had no intention of rushing to change over from the model that they already had in World Championship use. Since the two cars shared the same basic platform and running gear, when the time came to make the change, the team expected to be ready. In the meantime, for 1990, Carlos Sainz was the undisputed Number One driver, and all TTE's efforts went into propelling him towards a World Championship title.

Out on the stages, the battle with Lancia continued in the same way that 1989 had ended. In Monte Carlo, three TTE cars faced up to three Martini Lancias, and although Mazda and Mitsubishi were also present, they were only bit-part players. The 'old order,' in fact, had not changed, for at the front the battle was also Sainz versus Didier Auriol, with the lead changing hands no fewer than eleven times during the 26 special stage event. Toyota thought that Lancia's Deltas were cheating over the new turbocharger restriction regulations (but Toyota's time would come, in future years ...), though its protests were eventually rejected.

Even so, the competition was incredibly close, with Sainz only finally ceding the lead five stages from home, on the final night in the mountains, when the Lancia was, as we might say, 'suspiciously' fast compared with earlier sectors of the event. In the end the gap was just 52 seconds ...

With the Swedish rally most bizarrely cancelled because the weather was too mild (the organisers were not able to put on a competitive and safe event unless snow and ice could be guaranteed ...), there was a considerable gap until the rally teams started in Portugal, in March. Unhappily, as far as Toyota was concerned, this was a complete wipe-out, for Lancia finished 1-2-3-4-5, and both the 'works' Celicas retired, though the team's new recruit, Armin Schwarz, had led in the early stages, and Carlos Sainz had been leading at half distance. Schwarz eventually went off the road, and Sainz's rear transmission let him down.

On the original ST165-type, the engine bay of the 'works' rally cars was already well filled. This photograph was taken on the 1990 Monte Carlo Rally. At that time, as far as one can see, there was no strut bracing across the bay to stiffen the structure.

Hectic service point action on the Monte Carlo Rally of January 1990. That is Mikael Ericsson's car getting all the attention. Ericsson went on to finish seventh.

Carlos Sainz giving it everything in the 1990 Monte Carlo Rally, when he finished second overall, just 52 seconds behind Auriol's Lancia.

A tense moment, choosing tyres, during the brief halt en route. Carlos Sainz and Luis Moya are at the centre of the action, with team manager Maurice Guaslard looking over Moya's shoulder.

Things would have to improve soon – and in Africa they duly did. Not only did the 'old fox,' Björn Waldegård, win his fourth Safari in a Celica GT-Four, but team-mates Mikael Ericsson and Carlos Sainz took third and fourth places too. This, in fact, was originally meant to be Björn's final drive for Toyota (he had been connected with the team for sixteen years), as he was nearing his forty-seventh birthday, and was about to turn to desert 'Raid' rallies with Citroën.

Amazingly, this was the first occasion on which the Celica GT-Four had been used on a long-distance 'endurance' African Rally, so victory had not been expected, but merely hoped for! Much testing, of course, had been carried out in advance (mechanic, later team manager, George Donaldson was based in a Nairobi workshop almost full-time from October 1989), but since no-one really expected to win at first, against all the odds, this was a quite remarkable achievement.

Quite suddenly, it seemed, the Celica was now strong enough, and versatile enough, to tackle any World event, and stand a good chance of success, especially if Carlos Sainz was at the wheel. In Corsica, for instance, Sainz and Didier Auriol (Lancia Delta Integrale) fought tooth-and-nail for four days, with Sainz taking nine fastest stage times, and ten second fastests: though the Lancia won, it was only by 36 seconds, and all the signs were in place.

Sainz's first World victory (it had been long awaited) followed within weeks, when he won the rough-and-tumble Acropolis Rally, with team-mate, Mikael Ericsson, in fifth place. Not even his ex-team-mate, Juha Kankkunen (Lancia) could keep up with him. This was the big breakthrough. Once Carlos had won, he could look forward to winning again … and again … which is what duly happened.

Only one TTE made the long journey, half-way round the world, to New Zealand in June, but Sainz showed no signs of being lonely. Taking the lead at an early stage, he set no fewer than 27 fastest stage times (in a 43 stage event), but there were worrying moments along the way. In the first two days, a series of electrical problems caused him to lose ground, then have to make it up, but all was well from half-distance.

All, on the other hand, was *not* well in Argentina, where Carlos was once again sent off to compete on his own. According to the official results sheets, he took second place (behind Biasion's Lancia), and set eleven fastest stage times, and seventeen other 'podium' times – but this is to ignore the fact that he also rolled the car:

"The problem was that our notes were completely wrong. We had only checked the road twice, once in snow, and then in an ordinary rental car. Anyway, we crashed off the road and overturned three times. Fortunately we landed on our wheels ..." – the fact that they finished 27 minutes (minutes, not seconds) ahead of third-placed Didier Auriol, was scant compensation.

Björn Waldegård, a very seasoned campaigner in Africa, won the 1990 Safari Rally in this ST165. It was his last victory for the team.

Sometimes rallying isn't very glamorous – one of the 'works' GT-Fours trying to pick its way through deep, glutinous mud in the East African Safari of 1990, where team cars took first, third and fourth places.

Carlos Sainz and Luis Moya in the Tour de Corse in 1990, where they took second place, and gathered more points towards the Championship that would be theirs before the end of the season.

Once Carlos Sainz began winning for Toyota, he made a habit of it. In 1990 he became World Drivers' Champion – a season which included this victory in the Acropolis Rally.

Carlos Sainz won four World Championship events in 1990, this being the second, in New Zealand.

Every picture tells a story. In this case, during the Rally Argentina of 1990, Car No 1, driven by Carlos Sainz/Luis Moya, had already been damaged when it rolled in mid-stage, but mechanically there was little damage (except to the bodywork, and to the driver's self-esteem). In the end, Carlos took second place and set no fewer than eleven fastest stage times.

Sometimes it all goes wrong – like in Argentina 1990 when Carlos Sainz crashed his ST165 – though he still managed to finish second.

Then came the Finnish 1000 Lakes, that Finnish 'Grand Prix' which was thought to be so specialised that it only ever seemed to be won by a Scandinavian driver. Although the Swedish pilot, Mikael Ericsson (now a TTE driver), had won the event in 1989, for the previous decade it was the Finns who had won their own native event. Amazingly, in August 1990, Carlos Sainz, from Spain, turned that tradition on its head, not only winning the 1000 Lakes for the very first time, but by being consistently faster than the stellar line-up of Finns and Swedes behind him. Note the registration number of Sainz's car – K-AMK8139 – for this was a very significant, and very important, occasion.

No other non-Scandinavian finished in the top ten. Neither Mazda, with its latest enlarged-engined 323s, or Ford, with its newly-homologated Sierra Cosworth 4x4s, figured strongly in the results.

For this event, TTE had made a truly massive effort. Having chosen to enter just two cars – for Sainz and Ericsson – they settled on a well-proven 'gravel' specification (at least, they said they were, but since there was still an air of secrecy surrounding the team, as far as the specialist media was concerned, we never quite knew what novelties were hidden away), used the very latest Pirelli tyres, and settled on 16in wheels. As the 1989 winner, Ericsson started from No 1, with Sainz running No 4.

Even though there were 42 special stages, most of the 'works' drivers approached this 1000 Lakes as a four-day sprint. Markku Alen, who had more experience than anyone else in the field, always talked about 'Maximum Attack,' which was the agreed policy.

Although Sainz led almost all the way, he was lucky to start, for he had suffered a horrifying pre-start practice accident a few days before the 'off,' when his training car encountered two cars parked stationary across a stage – no-one ever owned up to the crime, the provenance of the cars could not be traced, but stupid anti-rallying 'Greens' were always suspected.

Although Juha Kankkunen's Lancia led at the end of the first day, Sainz was only two seconds behind him, and on the following morning soon took the lead and began to draw away. It was a three-man race for many hours – with Sainz, Kankkunen and Ari Vatanen (Mitsubishi Galant VR4) setting almost all the fastest times – before Kankkunen's Lancia broke a throttle linkage and lost several minutes, after which the second Celica driver settled into third place: but only until he rolled the car on Stage 21, and left Sainz to battle on, on his own.

In 1990, Carlos Sainz won three World rallies in ST165s – and gave a storming performance in the Finnish 1000 Lakes when he humbled all the local heroes.

The statistics, in the end, tell their own story – of 42 stages, Sainz was fastest on 23 of them, with Vatanen's Mitsubishi fastest 17 times, to finish second. At the finish, back in Laajavuori, the winning margin was just 19 seconds, but that was enough to send Sainz into automotive heaven, to confirm him at the head of the Drivers' Championship table, and to upset all the 'givens' in World rallying.

Not that the season was all over, for in Australia, Kankkunen (Lancia Integrale) fought back strongly to defeat Sainz by 1min 40sec. It was a long, hard-fought battle, for both drivers recorded fifteen fastest stage times, and virtually no-one was ever in the running to beat them. Both cars suffered from punctures, minor mishaps, and mechanical dramas, but neither had major accidents – such as that which eliminated rivals like Didier Auriol's Lancia.

With neither team then planning to tackle the unpopular Ivory Coast Rally, the final shoot-out was sure to come in Italy in the San Remo event. Three Celicas faced up to three full 'works' Lancias, several other 'supported' Integrales, and three 'works' Ford Sierra Cosworth 4x4s. Over five days there would be 35 stages (12 of them on tarmac, the rest on loose gravel), spectators crowds were enormous, and a great battle was forecast.

Carlos Sainz won the RAC Rally of 1990, using the ST165, which was fast becoming the most successful Group A car in World Championship rallies.

clinched the World Drivers' title, and performed many doughnuts with the Spanish flag fluttering across the roof of his also-mildly-damaged car.

Since Lancia had also clinched the Makes' title on San Remo, for both teams the RAC Rally was something of an 'end-of-term' party. Toyota pitched up with three 'works' cars (plus David Llewellin in his British-Championship car), while Lancia brought along two official Integrales, and gave support to cars from the Jolly Club.

As expected, this four-day/41 stage event was a forest-fest, and was dominated with what had become a familiar battle, season-long – between Carlos in a Celica, and Juha Kankkunen in an Integrale. With the exception of Kenneth Eriksson (Mitsubishi Galant VR4) no other individual or team looked like matching these two, who shared the lead almost throughout.

In the end, most of the fastest Finns suffered big accidents or had major mechanical failures – the list of 'DNF' included Hannu Mikkola, Markku Alen, Pentti Airikkala, Timo Salonen, Ari Vatanen and Juha Kankkunen – which left Sainz serenely in the lead, which he held to the very end. The gap, over second-place man Kenneth Eriksson, was 1min 42sec, enough if not completely emphatic. It was the sort of end-of-season climax which made every Toyota fan extremely happy.

This duly occurred, and although Toyota and Lancia both lost cars in the heat of battle, the fight was always between Sainz's Celica and Auriol and Kankkunen in Lancias: just a little further back, Mikael Ericsson's Celica would take sixth place. If you look at fastest stage times, the Celicas led the way – Sainz and Armin Schwarz set 14 FTDs between them – but on sheer consistency Lancia won the battle, with both Auriol and Kankkunen finishing just ahead of Carlos.

Schwarz's rally, unhappily, ended on the final day with his Celica hitting a tree stump – hard – but Carlos

Not only did Carlos Sainz (right) and Luis Moya win the 1990 RAC Rally, they also confirmed victory in the 1990 World Drivers' Rally Championship.

European and British series

In European Championship events, the big battle was still between Toyota, the Integrale (on all events), and the Ford Sierra RS Cosworth (on tarmac). TTE did not give as much support to its cars at this level as did Lancia or Ford, which may be one reason why GT-Fours notched up only four victories. In the British (Shell Open) Championship, David Llewellin won the series for the second year in succession, using a new Celica GT-Four. Four victories and one second place (which included success on the Circuit of Ireland and Ulster events, both of which were held on tarmac) emphasised just how good the driver, and his car, had now become.

The big story, of course, was that Carlos Sainz had become World Rally Champion for the first time. His first-ever World victory, in Greece in this momentous season, came only three years after he first started out in World events – yet during 1970 he had started eleven events, winning four times, and finishing second on another occasions.

Carlos intended to do this all again – and would do so, in 1992 – while Toyota still had to wait to win the Makes' series: Ove Andersson, though, was quite determined to do that …

During 1990, David Llewellin won four out of the seven British Championship rallies. Here, in F88 LPH, he took second place in the Cartel Rally – four outright victories would follow in the months to come.

Using the third of three GT-Fours prepared for him by Phil Collins' business, David Llewellin splashes his way towards victory in the Ulster Rally of 1970. His co-driver was Phil Short.

Mohammed Bin Sulayem was the dominant driver in the Middle East for years in the 1990s, usually with Ronan Morgan alongside him.

Is this a testing shot, for publicity purposes? The cleanliness of Mohammed Bin Sulayem's ST165 makes this likely.

1991

Even though the second-generation four-wheel-drive Celica GT-Four was being marketed throughout the year, TTE carried on using the existing ('old') ST165-type car throughout the 1991 season, by which time it was thoroughly proven, and a rally winner in almost every circumstance. Although Carlos Sainz would win no fewer than five World events, he could finish only second in the World Drivers' Championship, as his one-time team-mate Juha Kankkunen also won five times in Lancias, and had a slighter better run of minor placings!

For 1991 there was a re-shuffle of 'works' team drivers. Naturally, Carlos Sainz was the undisputed team leader (he would start no fewer than twelve World events), while Armin Schwarz started eight times (winning once – in Spain towards the end of the season). Mikael Ericsson, however, was no longer a regular member, starting just three events (he took second place on the Safari), and Björn Waldegård rejoined the team for just one event – his favourite, the Safari.

For Toyota, and Sainz, the 1991 seasons started well, with an unexpected victory on the Monte Carlo Rally. Such a win was fervently desired, of course, but even on the final night Sainz had seemed to be well beaten by Ford-debutant Delecour's Sierra Cosworth 4x4. Until, that is, the Ford suffered a broken suspension joint on the very last special stage, which relegated him to third place at the finish, in total despair.

For Toyota, a win was a win, gleefully accepted, especially as it had been longing for Monte success since Ove Andersson himself had begun driving Toyotas in the 1970s, but it was already clear that the battle with Lancia – for event wins and Championship titles – would be close-fought, all season. Not that this showed in Sweden, which did not count for the Makes' series, and which was therefore ignored by all the top teams.

In Portugal, in March, however, it was all very different – for two 'works' Toyotas faced two 'works' Lancias, with other well-backed 'private' cars of both marques, too. The Fords were a major disappointment, for all three of the Sierras were eliminated by accidents. The five-day event, held over 36 special stages, was a typically Iberian gravel stage spectacular, in which Carlos Sainz and both the leading Lancias (driven by Didier Auriol and Miki Biasion) fought it out, kilometre by kilometre.

Not only that, but TTE's second driver, Armin Schwarz, also held the lead for a time on the first day (he set four sparkling fastest stage times), until he went off the road on Stage 11, in foggy and increasingly slippery conditions. Carlos finally took the lead just before the end of the second day, then held it to the end, though never a long way ahead of the Lancias. Although he set fastest stage times on 18 (out of 36) occasions, it was close, the outcome being that the winning margin was only 47 seconds.

TTE, and Carlos, were now on something of a high – starting in Greece 1990 the combination had already won no fewer than six out of nine starts. Was this going to signal dominance of the World rally scene for the near future? TTE hoped that it would, but Lancia was determined that the balance should change – and it duly did as the season progressed.

The 'balance' duly came into play in Africa, at Eastertide, when the East African Safari took its usual toll on teams, and their much-strengthened cars. Although the Celica GT-Four had won the event at its first attempt in 1990, this was no guarantee of a trouble-free run in 1991 – and it was not. Toyota reshuffled its resources, resting Armin Schwarz, this time backing Sainz with Mikael Ericsson, and by that famous Safari stalwart Björn Waldegård.

Toyota was well prepared, for Ericsson had spent three months testing, to try to shake all the remaining bugs out of the Celica, and ensure that it was strong enough for this, the most demanding of World rallies. Not only had Björn won four previous Safaris, but three of those victories had been in Toyotas: Björn, in fact, had been competing in this event for nearly twenty years ...

This was, as usual, a phenomenally long, tough, and exhausting event. Sainz took the lead almost at once, then held it for the next four days, until he was cruelly eliminated on the penultimate day when his Toyota's engine suddenly failed, with a broken connecting rod. Although Waldegård

Was Armin Schwarz the most unlucky, or the most headstrong, of the Toyota 'works' drivers? He led the Tour de Corse twice in 1991, spun out several times, and eventually crashed his car. Ove Andersson was not impressed ...

finally finished fourth, he rolled his car at one point, and Mikael Ericsson, though second to the winning Lancia, had never actually been in the lead at all. It was a typical Safari in so many ways, for though Ericsson was second, he was 26 minutes behind the winner.

Normal service, as one might say, was then restored for TTE, when Sainz and Schwarz arrived in Corsica with tarmac-spec Celicas, and the very best of Pirelli tyres, to face up to three competitive Lancias over 27 stages of twisty, unrelentingly slow, tarmac stages. Except that

Ford's new man, Francois Delecour, was mesmerisingly fast (with his Sierra Cosworth 4x4) until half-distance, it was a two brand battle, which Sainz finally won on the last day. The winning margin over Auriol's Lancia was just 65 seconds, but Carlos set 12 fastest stage times to emphasise that his Celica was ideal for these conditions. Unhappily, Schwarz crashed – again – which for a time led to rumours that he was to be sacked from the team. Toyota, however, remained loyal to him, and his fortunes duly changed.

Rallying at its most pleasant, and most exciting – but the author cannot 'place' the shot. The driver is Carlos Sainz and the year is 1990 or 1991, when the ST165 was at its best.

In Greece, on the Acropolis, in June, Toyota wanted to repeat its Sainz victory of 1990, but could not quite pull it off. The big news of this event was that organisation seemed to be sadly lacking (Carlos called it a 'Mickey Mouse' rally, and, like several of his rivals, almost suffered from crashes with non-competing cars that had strayed on to the routes). The sensation – to be accurate, the unlucky sensation – of the event, was Kenneth Eriksson's new-type Mitsubishi Galant VR4: although it set far more fastest stage times than any rival, it never actually led the rally, as an early road penalty put Eriksson towards the back of the field, and a late crash did him no favours either.

Neither Sainz nor his major rivals, Didier Auriol and Juha Kankkunen in Lancias, needed to match those times, though the lead changed repeatedly during the four days and 47 stages in hot and dusty conditions. Sainz finally ceded the lead to Kankkunen on the last day, and ended up second, just 61 seconds behind him.

It was all very close now, and the see-saw continued to operate when Sainz beat Kankkunen by just 75 seconds in New Zealand, and Didier Auriol was close behind them both, just as he had been in Greece. Once again, the stats tell a story, for of the 40 stages which spanned five days, Sainz was fastest on 20 of them, Auriol was fastest 14 times, and Kankkunen seven times – yet Juha was more consistent when it came to setting second and third fastest times. Sainz, though, led the rally from start to finish, and never really looked likely to be beaten. Modern Group A rally cars seemed to be becoming so reliable, and the service umbrellas so efficient, that every world-class driver could drive flat-out, most of the time, without worrying about breakages: this trend was soon reversed, as the team's experiences in Argentina would show.

No time to look at the splendid scenery in New Zealand in 1991, for Carlos Sainz was on his way to victory, a repeat of his 1990 performance.

Carlos Sainz used K-AM7878 to win the Rally of New Zealand in 1991. If identities mean anything (and we cannot be certain!) this same car had already won the British RAC Rally at the end of 1990.

The hardened professionals then all trekked around the Southern Hemisphere, from New Zealand to Argentina, where three Celicas faced up to no fewer than four official Lancias, and two well supported 'private' examples from the Astra SRL organisation. Although Celica sales in Argentina (in South America, even) were still quite restricted, this event was not only a World qualifier, but was also thought to be a good 'headline' event for the world of motoring to admire the cars.

According to the registration number carried (K-AM1457), Carlos had yet another brand-new Celica for the occasion, and used it to the best possible advantage, though on this occasion he had to fight longer, and harder, to gain the final advantages. Though the other two cars, driven by Mikael Ericsson and Mohammed Bin Sulayem, could not match the phalanx of Lancias, Carlos set 13 fastest times (out of 29 stages in all), and finally won the event by just eight nail-biting seconds. Not that it was an easy victory, for Carlos's car punctured and broke a wheel at one stage (this dropped him to fifth), and ended another stage with a serious engine oil loss, which was successfully staunched. The Lancias, similarly had steering, driveshaft and turbo breakages …

Finally, as Martin Holmes commented in *World Rallying 14*: "Coming into the stadium at Cordoba after the final control he [Sainz] carried out his usual spin turns

In the early 1990s, there were times when the Toyota plus Sainz combination was almost unbeatable unless mechanical disaster struck. This was the Argentine Rally in 1991, which Carlos won, beating an entire fleet of 'works' Lancias in the process.

in front of the crowds and promptly broke his gearbox ... Photographers who watched him reverse round the perimeter track and go up the finish ramp backwards thought it was a bad joke on the Spaniard's part, but his shrug of the shoulders tried to tell them it wasn't intentional."

With Toyota only a handful of points ahead of Lancia, the pressure was there, almost tangible.

It was in Finland that everything started to go wrong with the rest of Toyota's season, for neither Carlos Sainz, nor TTE itself, would win another event in 1991. In the end, and unhappily for Toyota's 'face' Lancia would win all four remaining events. It was not that the Italians suddenly had the better car, but that Toyota's luck seemed to have run out for the time being.

Carlos Sainz's GT-Four retired from Spain 1991, which left team-mate Armin Schwarz to battle for, and win, the event. He set nine fastest stage times.

This is what happened in Finland. Although Carlos had another brand-new car to use, and set by far the most fastest stage times, he could only finish fourth, three minutes behind Kankkunen. The reason? As quoted in the *Autosport* report of the event: "On the final stage of the day [SS34, in fact], it all changed. Sainz flew over a crest flat in sixth gear, landed off the road, bounced back, and then spun into a ditch. In a cloud of steam (probably as much from the cockpit as from the wrecked front of the Toyota), he limped to the finish, the engine out of water and overtaken by Kankkunen."

In terms of the World Championship, it all seemed to be worth it, as at this point Sainz was well ahead of Juha Kankkunen, and Toyota was just shading Lancia in the Makes' series. All that, though, was about to change ...

Even so, in this most frantic of seasons, there was to be no 'summer holiday' for Toyota. Having sent 'works' cars to Corsica (May), Acropolis (June), New Zealand (also June) and Argentina (July), in August they were faced with doing battle once again, with Lancia and Mitsubishi in Finland! Three cars – for Sainz, Schwarz and (Toyota-Sweden car) Mats Jonsson would face two Lancias and two Mitsubishis.

After frantic repair work from TTE technicians: "The front of the car had to be straightened with ropes and jacks, while tie wraps held the new radiator and fans in place" – this allowed the car to limp to the end of the day, with further work being carried out overnight.

This, though, was nothing compared with what was to unfold in Australia a few weeks later. TTE sent three cars – two of them brand-new – to contest the Perth-based event, but found the Lancias better prepared, and better suited to the specific gravel stages of Western Australia. Although Sainz was competitive (when was he *not* competitive …?), he threw it all away on SS14. Coming into view in a spectator area at high speeds, he cut a corner too sharply, the car was instantly pitched into a roll, and proceeded to barrel roll no fewer than seven times (counted on video taken of the accident), before coming to rest, totally wrecked. Fortunately neither Carlos nor his co-driver, Luis Moya, suffered more than a thorough fright and shaking up. Team-mate Armin Schwarz was mentally shaken by all this, though he still set six fastest stage times, before finishing third overall.

Back in Europe, would there be a change of fortune on San Remo? Up to a point, yes, though the impetus seemed to have been knocked out of TTE for a time. The basic results show that Sainz finished sixth overall, which was a disappointment by any normal TTE standards – while he set 11 fastest stage times. The problem was that not only was Carlos feeling stiff and sorry for himself after Australia, but the transmission of his GT-Four failed catastrophically, and needed to be changed: this caused him to lose 13 minutes on the road, and drop him right out of contention.

With only two events still to go in the season, Lancia seemed certain to take the Makes' series again, while Sainz's lead over Juha Kankkunen was looking very creaky. What happened in Spain (which did not count for the Makes' Series in 1991) would be important, therefore.

For Carlos, a shoot-out in Spain, his home country, looked ideal. Although he had not yet won this event (this was the rally's first World appearance, by the way), he had the backing of millions of Spaniards, and was confident. Toyota sent two cars – for Sainz and Schwarz – while Lancia sent Juha Kankkunen on his own. Somehow, though, it all went wrong, immediately. On the first day, after six stages, instead of Sainz it was team-mate Schwarz who led the event, and on the second morning Sainz found that his car would simply not fire up in Parc Ferme, and he never took the re-start. Schwarz, in spite of a roll, and in spite of needing a gearbox change on the final morning, finally took the tarmac victory that many had expected of him for so long.

In the end, therefore, the World Championships were not finally settled until the last event of the year – the British RAC Rally. Toyota, disappointed, if not entirely disheartened by the awful fortune they had suffered in recent months, chopped their entry, so that only one official car – naturally for Carlos Sainz – took the start. This, in fact, was to be the very last World Rally TTE was to tackle in the original ST165 model, for building of new ST185-type 'works' cars had already begun in Cologne.

The story of the RAC Rally is easily told. The Lancias (which were widely suspected of using 'special' fuel additives …) were quicker than Sainz's Toyota throughout. Carlos led, very briefing, in mid-rally, but set only five fastest times out of 37 special stages. His Celica gave much more trouble than usual – for the engine began to overheat persistently, which meant that the cylinder head gasket had to be changed (miraculously this was done without incurring road penalties) – and in the end he had to settle for a rather disgruntled third place overall.

Accordingly, at the end of an exciting season, in which fortunes swung one way, then the other, Carlos and Lancia rival Juha Kankkunen both won five rallies, but Kankkunen eventually beat Carlos to the Championship crown by seven points. In the Makes' series of ten events, Toyota had won four times, and Lancia six times, which allowed the Italians to take that Championship quite comfortably.

European and British events

In view of the cars' performances at World level, it was no doubt disappointing to TTE that the Celica won only two European Championship rounds during the year – once in Sweden, and once in Portugal. Even in Britain, where David Llewellin had once quite dominated rallying with his GT-Four, there were no successes to report, for Llewellin had moved on to another team, and no other driver had risen to take his place.

1992

Major changes for 1992 included concentration on the new-type ST185 model (which, as has already been noted in the 'Car and team' section, was a troublesome beast at first), and on the addition of rally veteran Markku Alen to the team, to join Carlos Sainz and Armin Schwarz. The team continued to expand in many ways, for this was the height of the service cars + chase cars + helicopters + aircraft period. One planning complication was that for this season the FIA specified that no driver could tackle more than ten of the

Although he was not a member of the TTE 'World' team, Mohammed Bin Sulayem (right), along with Ronan Morgan, was dominant for Toyota in Middle East rallying for some years.

Markku Alen drove for TTE during the 1992 season.

fourteen qualifying events – which caused Carlos Sainz to miss out on events he might have preferred to start.

As for some years, most of the head-to-head competition came from Lancia, but when the Delta Integrales were running in strictly sporting-legal form (this did not always seem to happen …) they were now seen to be past their best: it cannot have helped that Lancia 'officially' withdrew from competition, handing over its cars and its Martini sponsorship to the Jolly Club in their place. Ford, on the other hand, had finally sorted out its bulky Sierra Cosworth 4x4s: this and the fact that Miki Biasion had joined its team, made Ford serious competitors at last, though it never quite achieved lasting and outright success.

Although Carlos Sainz finished second in Monte Carlo, just 125 seconds behind Auriol's Lancia, it hid a noticeable gap in performance, for Auriol's car set many more fastest stage times. Not only that, but both Alen and Schwarz crashed their cars (Schwarz was becoming very consistent in leaving battered Celicas behind him though, in fairness, he set five fastest stage times and led the event at first …), so there was still much to do.

Toyota began using the new-style ST185 in 1992. On the car's first outing, Monte Carlo, Carlos Sainz finished second, and started out on the path to World Champion for the second time.

Only three weeks later, Mats Jonsson brought joy and a modicum of embarrassment to TTE when he won the Swedish Rally outright. Joy for the obvious reasons, but embarrassment, not only because he was entered by Toyota-Sweden, but the car was an old-type ST165, and the tyres were by Michelin. Also driving Toyota-Sweden ST165 cars were Markku Alen (fourth) and Leif Asterhag (fifth), but there was no sign of the new-type ST185s from Cologne, nor of team-leader Carlos Sainz.

TTE began using the ST185 in 1992, where Carlos Sainz took second place in Monte Carlo. This was Armin Schwarz who – guess what? – later had an accident …

Markku Alen's car being serviced, outdoors, in the 1992 Swedish Rally. (Reproduced from the BP/Castrol Archive)

In the Swedish Rally of 1992, Leif Asterhag took fifth place in this privately-supported ST165 – which was about to be replaced by the new type ST185. (Reproduced from the BP/Castrol Archive)

Then came Portugal, where TTE was back with a vengeance, not only producing three ST185s, but their A-team of Sainz, Schwarz and Alen. Unhappily, Schwarz crashed – again, this was getting too regular for Ove Andersson's liking – and while Markku Alen set more fastest stage times than Sainz, he suffered a driveshaft failure at one point which cut his chances. Sainz's car also blew a turbocharger at one point too, so in the end it was Juha Kankkunen's Lancia consistency (and, to be fair, a series of stupendously impressive stage times) which gave him the victory. Miki Biasion's second place in a 'works' Sierra surprised everyone, and the TTE cars had to settle for third and fourth.

Meantime, and back at Cologne, TTE had been preparing a massive attack on the Safari Rally, an event that Toyota had already won four times in the previous decade. Three new ST185s were joined by several old-style ST165s in private hands, with major 'works' competition coming only from Lancia, this looked like a serious effort from Toyota.

Although Lancia fought hard, this was an event almost made for Carlos Sainz to win – which he duly did, actually leading at the vast majority of time controls. The huge team was in high spirits – at one point Carlos's car suffered a turbo failure, Carlos asked for a change, and the work was duly completed in just eight minutes. In the end he defeated Kankkunen's Lancia by a massive 52 minutes, with Mikael Ericsson (who had done much of the pre-event testing) fourth and Markku Alen fifth, after he rolled his car when the route was obscured by thick dust. This was an astonishing performance for a car (a bodyshell type, really) which was brand-new to Africa.

Lighter and more developed new cars appeared in Corsica in May, using the newly-developed tubular-frame rear suspension subframes for the very first time. Two ST185s took the start (Sainz and Schwarz) but, despite their collective experience, could not keep up with the Lancias, or even with Francois Delecour's flying Sierra. Not a single fastest stage was achieved, for Sainz's fourth place was credited to the gritty consistency of the Spaniard.

Carlos took fourth in the 1992 Tour de Corse in the rapidly improving ST185-type.

Could things get any worse for TTE in the Acropolis, which the Celica had previously won in 1990? Indeed it could, because all the team cars suffered from repeated turbocharger failures, and in the end all three cars – Sainz, Alen and Schwarz – all crashed out of the event. Sainz's car was on its roof, the other cars both crashed on the same corner and ended up nestling close to each other, a long way off a rough Greek track.

Because of this TTE, who (for financial reasons) had been hoping not to go to New Zealand and to Argentina, now felt obliged to do so to keep its (and Sainz's) Championship hopes alive. Just one car was prepared and hastily air-freighted out to Auckland where, in the end, Sainz had to face up to a fleet of Subaru Legacy-types, but no Martini/Jolly Club Lancias and no Fords. In the end it was almost a hollow victory, for every single one of the Subarus suffered engine

Markku Alen drove several events for Toyota in 1992, including the Acropolis Rally. Unhappily, every TTE team car crashed out of this event.

A bad day at the office. In the Acropolis of 1992, all three GT-Four team cars crashed out of the rally – those of Alen and Schwarz (No 10) on the very same corner.

Carlos Sainz and Toyota came to love New Zealand. Here, in 1992, Carlos is on his way to victory in his ST185, dominating from start to finish, and recording his hat-trick of wins in the event.

failure, Sainz set the majority of fastest stages times, and his winning margin (over Liatti's ART-entered Lancia) was a comfortable four minutes 30 seconds.

Four weeks later it was almost, but not the same, story in Argentina, where TTE sent out a new car for Carlos Sainz to drive, and was faced with battling against several competitive Lancias, including those of Auriol (Martini car) and Alex Fiorio (Astra SRL team). In the end this developed into a straight fight between Carlos and Auriol, with the Celica having to settle for second place. The race for Championships was *still* wide open ...

Because of the 'ten events' limitation, Sainz then had to miss the Finnish 1000 Lakes Rally, where TTE was represented by Markku Alen and the young Marcus Gronholm. However, not even Markku, who seemed to have been a 1000 Lakes favourite since the mid-1970s, with the Fiat 131 Abarth, could match the pace of Auriol's Lancia: the handling was still a problem, as proved by Finnish radar guns which showed the Celica to be substantially fastest in a straight line, but not around the corners. Third for Alen was a brave effort, but he could not win the event.

Somehow, it seemed, this was not to be TTE's year, for in another long and gruelling trip Down Under, to Australia, just one new car was entered for Carlo Sainz, but he found he was simply not able to match the pace of the Lancias,

1000 Lakes Rally in 1992, with Markku Alen on his way to third place overall. (Courtesy Phil Short)

The importance of this result was not that Carlos won in front of his fans, but that he took the lead in the World Drivers' Championship just – but only just – ahead of Auriol and Kankkunen. Now it would all come down to a shoot-out on the British RAC Rally, which followed only days later, in November.

For Carlos and, as it transpired, his current career with Toyota, the dream came true in Chester at the end of a gruelling, 33 stage, RAC Rally. Not only did Carlos win the event outright – by 3min 16sec from Ari Vatanen's 'works' Subaru Legacy – but his Championship rivals both hit trouble. Because Juha Kankkunen's Lancia finished third, while Didier Auriol's sister Lancia stopped in mid-stage at

No luck for Armin Schwarz in Spain 1992, where he finished fifth in this high-flying GT-Four, though team-mate Carlos Sainz won the event.

the problem being one of handling, rather than of outright performance. The stats tell their own story, with Sainz taking just seven fastest stage times, but with the Auriol/Kankkunen Lancia steamroller taking 31 fastests.

The team then gave the San Remo and Bandama rallies a miss before sending Carlos Sainz and Armin Schwarz to tackle the Spanish Catalunya Rally, where Sainz was among millions of devoted, fanatical, followers. They were not disappointed. Didier Auriol threw away his chances by crashing his Lancia Integrale, leaving Carlos well in charge of the event, which he won in fine style from a fleet of other Lancias – and Armin Schwarz took sixth place.

It was the end of an eventful, sometimes frustrating, but finally successful season.

European events

Although TTE was still too involved in its own World programme to take too much interest in the European Rally Championship, in 1992 there were no fewer than six outright victories to Celica GT-Fours, one of them (Jonsson in South Sweden) being in the new-shape ST185 model. Toyota-GB, on the other hand, was no longer interested in the British series, and there were no successes for Celica models.

1993

As already mentioned, because Castrol arrived as a major sponsor to the team for 1993 and beyond, Carlos Sainz and Repsol (the Spanish oil company) were obliged to leave. In his place, TTE signed up the French driver Didier Auriol

Armin Schwarz was at once the unluckiest, and at times the most destructive, of 'works' drivers in the Toyota Celicas. Here is his ST185 at an early stage of the 1992 Catalunya Rally, in which he took fifth place. (Courtesy Phil Short)

a late juncture, with problems in the engine bay, Sainz was confirmed as the 1992 World Rally Champion. Although it was a convincing win, Sainz set only six fastest stage times, with both Colin McRae (Subaru) and Malcolm Wilson (Ford Sierra) out-gunning him on that score. Carlos, though, never put a foot wrong, and led the event from half-distance to the end.

The final wrinkle in weeks of behind-the-scenes negotiations came immediately after the RAC Rally, when new Champion, Carlos Sainz, confirmed that he would leave the team with immediate effect, a shock which Ove Andersson countered by signing up Juha Kankkunen, confirming sponsorship from Castrol, *and* revealing that he had signed up with Michelin, in place of Pirelli.

(who had recently battled with Sainz for the Drivers' World Championship) and, in another surprise signing, Juha Kankkunen returned to the team. Neither Armin Schwarz nor Markku Alen figured in the regular line-up of the re-jigged team, though Markku and other well respected names 'guested' for TTE on specific events.

To be brutally honest, this was the first year in which mutterings from other rival teams – and from independent reporters – began to suggest that TTE was not above indulging in sharp practice. Although everyone, without exception, liked team principal Ove Andersson, and his very experienced team manager, Phil Short, there were too many occasions when their cars seemed to be suspiciously fast, or the team cruised up to the very limit of the regulations.

Early in the year, as an example, Auriol's pace on the final night of the Monte Carlo Rally was – literally – unbelievable, while in Sweden excuses offered for the provision of replenishment oil in a banned place were difficult to support. Auriol himself was clearly an inventive influence on all such matters, and on all cars he drove, for controversy seemed to follow him from year to year: the 'cheating Toyota' syndrome, however, would not finally boil over until 1995.

The season started with high drama, and in controversial times. Almost everything about the rally 'circus' was new, including the appearance of new TTE drivers, new Escort RS Cosworths, and the new Mitsubishi Lancer. With only one night, and five stages to go, Ford's Francois Delecour was leading comfortably, but in the final stages Auriol's Celica GT-Four put on bursts of unbelievable speed, beating the Escort by 25 seconds over St Sauveur, 31 seconds over the Col de Felines, and 22 seconds over the sinuous Quartre Chemins.

Finally, Auriol beat the Ford by just 15 seconds. Writing in *Autosport*, Keith Oswin was not impressed:

"Rumours spread like wildfire. Was there something odd about the last night's turbo change? Was there any truth in stories of dubious fluids in the washer bottles allegedly plumbed to the engine via an extra injector? Does anyone really know what happened on the final stages to let Auriol find that extra turn of speed …?"

Series organisers clearly thought something had been done, but could not pin-point it at the time. It tells us much about their attitude that when, on the next event, in Sweden, Auriol just 'happened' to need engine oil, and 'found' some in a no-servicing area of the event, he was swiftly disqualified from the event (though his engine would probably not have made it to the end), and TTE was subsequently fined a massive $300,000, which was a world record rally fine at this moment in history. Faced with all this controversy, Toyota followers nearly missed the fact that Mats Jonsson won the event, and Juha Kankkunen took second place. Although Auriol had set more fastest stage times than either of them, he was banished before the end of the event.

It was a controversial way to start the season, and pressure on TTE intensified when the team chose to ignore Portugal, where Ford's new Escort took first and second places. Then, of course, came the Safari, and the most emphatic victory of all time. As ever, TTE had been testing and developing in Kenya for months before this Easter classic, and entered no fewer than three brand-new Celicas, to be driven by Juha Kankkunen, Markku Alen and Ian Duncan, with Yasuhiro Iwase driving an ex-Acropolis car from 1992: Didier Auriol was 'rested.'

The photographer took ages to find a Kenyan vantage point on the 1993 Safari where the 'works' ST185 would leap very high, at top speed. This was Juha Kankkunen, on his way to outright victory.

Although Toyota was the only top team that opted to take part (Ford and Mitsubishi stayed at home, and Carlos Sainz's small Lancia team could not justify the funds), it was as serious as ever, setting its stamp on the event from the early hours, and absolutely dominated the results. Though Ian Duncan's car was delayed when it hit an animal, no other marque ever headed the event, and Kankkunen led the whole way. In the end, the two Flying Finns – Kankkunen and Alen – were way out in front.

To quote Juha: "The Safari is never an easy event to win, but sometimes when everything goes well it feels easy. This time everything worked really well …"

Not that it was always going to be so easy, as TTE soon found out in Corsica in May. Not only was the Celica not yet rallying's quickest 'tarmac' car, but Ford had Francois Delecour and brand-new Escort RS Cosworths, and both were using the latest type of Michelin tyres. Even though there was

This magnificently posed, and purposeful, before-event team shot on the 1993 Safari shows just what sort of effort Toyota put into its programme at the time. Four ST185 driven (left to right) by Juha Kankkunen, Markku Alen, Ian Duncan and Yasuhiro Iwase, ready to take the four leading places in the event, which Kankkunen won outright.

dry, then wet, then once again dry conditions, the results told a very simple story – that Delecour led this tarmac event from start to finish – all 24 stages – while Didier Auriol and Francois Chatriot battled gamely on, ready to take over if the flying Frenchman ever made a mistake. Not that he did, the losing gap was just 62 seconds, and Ford thought it had got some recompense for the controversy of Monte Carlo.

Would fortunes change in Greece, on the Acropolis, where something like Safari conditions, but at even more intense speeds, would apply? TTE entered the 'A-Team' – Auriol and Kankkunen – and thought that they could. Facing them were Fords, Mitsubishis, Subarus, and even three cars from Italy's Jolly Club, which was rapidly running through its stock of ex-works Lancias! No matter – the Celica had won on Safari, so surely it could do it again?

The results showed, unhappily, that the team could not, for no Toyota ever led the 1993 Acropolis, and neither of the two team cars made it to the finish. First of all Auriol smashed his car's engine sump, which let out all the oil: later he went off the road again, damaging the engine cooling fans, and finally cooking the motor. Kankkunen, on the other hand, kept going in the face of a myriad of engine management system problems, until one final breakdown put him out of time limits. There was misery back in Cologne, and not without reason.

Things could only get better ... but in Argentina a personal trauma overshadowed everything TTE could do. Just before the event, Juha Kankkunen's co-driver, Juha Piironen, collapsed with a brain haemorrhage (from which, thankfully, he recovered, but became wheelchair bound), and Nicky Grist was drafted in as a last-minute replacement, by arrangement with Mitsubishi, with whom he was contracted. Amazingly, and in spite of this personal and sporting trauma, Kankkunen went on to win this demanding event, where hanging dust on all the stages meant that to start from the

Juha Piironen was Juha Kankkunen's regular co-driver until mid-1993, when he suffered a brain haemorrhage just before the Rally of Argentina. Happily, he recovered, but did no more rallying.

front, and run at the front, helped him enormously. It was Toyota's thirtieth World Rally victory, and well deserved, particularly as Didier Auriol's sister car also took third place in spite of struggling with a faulty gearbox for some time.

Things didn't go quite so well in New Zealand, where Auriol took third, and Kankkunen took fifth places, for this was an event where Colin McRae took his first World victory (in a Subaru Legacy), only 29 seconds ahead of Didier, so TTE looked forward eagerly to getting back to Europe, to tackle the 1000 Lakes.

Pre-event, all the headlines were about drivers, and not the cars. Not only did Kankkunen have yet another new co-driver – Dennis Giraudet (for Nicky Grist was not available) – but a third 'works' TTE Celica was to be driven by Hannu Mikkola, who was to make a one-off swansong appearance on the event which he had first won (in a Ford Escort Twin-Cam) way back in 1968! Toyota meant business – not only because it brought along three brand-new GT-Fours, but because it was running an early-generation traction control system on Mikkola's example.

By the early 1990s, the Toyota was supremely fast on all types of gravel rally, notably here in Argentina in 1993. Although Juha Kankkunen won the event, his team-mate, Didier Auriol, seen here, could only finish third after suffering transmission problems throughout.

On his way to the World Championship of 1993, Juha Kankkunen won five World events, and was well placed in several others – including fifth in this ST185 in the Rally of New Zealand. (Reproduced from the BP/Castrol Archive)

The result was a triumph for all concerned. Not only did Kankkunen win the event (but only narrowly, from Ari Vatanen's new-type Subaru Impreza), with Auriol third and Mikkola eighth, but this gave Juha a widening lead in the Drivers' Championship, and Toyota a good cushion (over Ford) in the Makes' series. All of which made another long trek halfway around the world (to Australia) a lot easier to face.

Not only did Juha win once again – after 34 stages, his winning margin over Vatanen's Subaru Legacy was a very comfortable six minutes – but this also confirmed Toyota's victory in the Makes' Championship for 1993 – its first ever, in fact the first ever by a Japanese brand. Didier Auriol, on the other hand, lasted only for six stages before his car hit a rock which had been flung into the road, which ripped off his sump, letting out all the oil and immediately cooking the engine.

Having sat out the San Remo Rally (with one Championship won, the other looking good for completion at the end of the year – and in any case Kankkunen didn't really enjoy tarmac events), TTE could then concentrate on the last two rallies of the year – the all-tarmac Catalunya Rally in Spain, and the mostly-gravel RAC Rally.

Based on Lloret de Mar, in 1993 the Catalunya was an all-tarmac event which should have seen the Spaniard (Carlos Sainz) fighting with his old team (Toyota) for the honours, but someone forgot this when writing the script, the result being that Francois Delecour's Ford Escort RS Cosworth lead almost the whole way, and won the event. Toyota beat every other car in the event, with Didier Auriol finishing second, exactly one minute behind Delecour, and Kankkunen more than three minutes further back. Not that Juha minded too much, for this confirmed him as Drivers' World Champion for 1993, and Toyota also looked sure to take the Makes' crown too.

And so they did on the RAC Rally, which followed just three weeks later. As if we hadn't guessed, it immediately became clear that TTE would be running new-shape ST205s at some point in 1994, for the team turned up in Birmingham with three already-used ST185s: Champion-elect Kankkunen had the car which won the 1000 Lakes, while Auriol had the car which had blown its engine in Australia. However, though this seemed like a case of 'using up old stock,' the GT-Fours were still immaculate, and still set all the standards for this snowy, 35 stage event.

Carrying the competition No 6, on an event sponsored by 'Telecom,' this was the Rally of Australia in 1993. Juha Kankkunen and Nicky Grist won the event comfortably, by six minutes from Ari Vatanen's Subaru Legacy.

Winners yet again! Juha Kankkunen (right) and Nicky Grist on the podium, after winning the Rally Catalunya in 1993. (Reproduced from the BP/Castrol Archive)

Time for a rest! Cleaned up after a phenomenal effort and on show many months later, this ST185, as driven by Juha Kankkunen to win the 1993 RAC Rally, takes centre stage. The Castrol plus Michelin sponsorship had been new for the 1993 season.

Once again, Auriol showed his dislike of British forests by setting only one fastest stage time, but Kankkunen, looking amazingly relaxed at all times, battled for the lead throughout, saw Colin McRae's new Subaru ahead of him for three stages on the third morning, then held the lead serenely to the end, beating Kenneth Eriksson's Mitsubishi Lancer Evolution by more than two minutes. Need I say that this was enough to ensure that Toyota would also win the Makes' season, which sealed a remarkable season for the Cologne-based outfit.

Was it any wonder that Juha's still new co-driver, Nicky Grist, had this to say at the press conference after the finish:

"What can you say about a man with four World Championships, who has won more Championship rallies than anyone else? The way Juha's driving at the moment, I think he'll just go on and on. He's simply the best – that's all you can say …"

European Championship events

Because 1993 was the 'year of the Escort Cosworth,' when many owners took advantage of Ford's amazingly efficient Group A parts-supply systems, there were few Toyota victories at European Championship level. Nevertheless, 'works'-supported ST185s won four events outright – twice for Mats Jonsson, and twice for Franz Wittman.

1994

Right from the start of the year, Toyota set out a clear strategy for its World Rally programme. Juha Kankkunen and Didier Auriol remained, as its leading drivers, while other drivers (including Andrea Aghini from Italy) were used less frequently. Marc Duez became chief test driver, but did not feature in the rallying strength. The team used the well-proven (if sometimes recalcitrant) ST185 models for much of the year, though the new-style ST205 made its first appearance (as a Group N car) in the Finnish 1000 Lakes, then as a Group A car in Australia.

The result was almost a repeat performance of 1993, with Toyota once again winning the Makes' Championship (comfortably, as it happened, from Subaru), with Didier Auriol winning the Drivers' Championship and Juha Kankkunen third. This was a year in which Auriol won three times, and Kankkunen just once.

Two surprisingly heavy brand-new cars started in Monte Carlo, both of them fitted with the latest level of traction control equipment, which could be switched off if the drivers thought it wasn't working for them. Although Auriol led briefly, he then went off the road, his car being too badly damaged to be recovered. Kankkunen also went off the road avoiding errant spectators, his ST185 suffering panel damage. In the end, Juha took second place, just 65 seconds (in 22 stages) behind Delecour's winning Ford Escort RS Cosworth.

Because of the way the 1994 Championship was structured, the Swedish only counted for points if one drove a 2-litre front-wheel-drive car ('Formula 2'), so Toyota did not send 'works' cars. Instead, local hero Thomas Radstrom had a private ST185, with support from Toyota-Sweden – which was quite enough for him to win the event outright.

Toyota, it seemed, was quite determined to win the World series in 1994, almost without regard to costs. For Portugal, where Kankkunen's gravel-driving skills would be paramount, the team produced yet another two brand-new ST185 cars, though Andrea Aghini had to make do with a machine once rallied by Auriol in Argentina. Traction control, still under development, was once again a feature of the cars, which were still improving in so many small ways. Although Delecour's Ford Escort RS Cosworth led the event at first, after its engine let go Kankkunen moved smoothly into the lead. At the end of the event, after thirty-six special stages, Juha had set nine fastest times, Didier Auriol ten fastest times, yet Juha won the event by just 40 seconds: Aghini, still familiarising himself with his new car (he had previously been a Lancia specialist) crashed.

Then came Toyota's habitual assault on the Safari, where no fewer than four specially-honed ST185s had been entered, backed by several privately entered examples. George Donaldson had been running a special development and testing workshop in Nairobi for some time, and before the start the team was considered to be virtually unbeatable.

This startling shot confirms just how much effort TTE put into making specialised GT-Fours for the Safari Rally. For 1994, the cars had features such as moulded air intakes for the engine, extra driving lamps at the base of the screen pillars, sturdy animal crash bars around the nose, and a mounting for an extra spare wheel on the outside of the hatch. Ian Duncan won the event that year. This car was driven by Juha Kankkunen, who suffered a terrifying high speed crash.

The team's publicity chief was proud to admit it had hired a massive Russian Antonov freight aircraft to carry 100 tons of cars, wheels, tyres and other equipment to Africa from Germany – plus Michael Kahlfuss's tiny Trabant 601R!

The results, in fact, showed that no non-Celica driver led the event at any time. However, as far as the Safari was concerned, it was never wise to make assumptions – for as it happened, only two of the four cars would make it to the finish, the event was won by the team's only local driver (Ian Duncan), and Juha Kankkunen was involved in a most unpleasant accident, which team manager Phil Short thinks had a long-term effect on his capabilities and approach to the sport.

Three of the cars were brand-new ST185 'heavyweights,' with Yoshio Fujimoto being allocated a refurbished test car. Didier Auriol led at first until his car suffered shock absorber, steering, then driveshaft failures, after which Safari veteran Kankkunen took over and began to pull away. Then came near tragedy in the Taita Hills, when, according to team manager Phil Short:

"Juha hit a 'washaway' at high speed, unaware of its presence. Marc Duez had been driving our course checking car but, when he arrived at the spot there was so much dust from passing traffic that he had to slow down to walking pace and simply didn't realise that it was there. There was a further complication in that the radio link to our communications plane wasn't working at the time, so everything that could have gone wrong did …"

Juha hit the washaway at very high speed, barrel-rolled the car, completely destroyed it, and was obliged to go to the nearest hospital for tests. Juha suffered cuts to his hand, co-driver Nicky Grist broke a bone in his hand but, miraculously, both were able to take part in the Tour de Corse just four weeks later. Local hero Ian Duncan admitted that if he had been running in such conditions, without being warned, that he would very likely have suffered the same fate – but was able to keep going, winning the rally by 25 minutes from Shinozuka's Mitsubishi, with Didier Auriol's ST185 a further 45 minutes away in third place.

May brought concerns for Toyota, for (as already stated) its team principal Ove Andersson was currently hospitalised after a heart bypass operation), while its No 1 driver, Juha Kankkunen, initially seemed to be completely un-nerved by the high-speed accident in Kenya. At the same time, May also brought the traumatising news of Ayrton Senna's tragic death in the F1 San Marino GP, and the FIA's proposals to ban four-wheel-drive cars from rallying after 1996.

For Toyota, though, there was an immediate change of fortune in the Tour de Corse. Although Ford's Escort RS Cosworths would have started as favourites, its star driver, Francois Delecour, was in dock with badly smashed ankles following a non-rallying car accident in northern France, which meant that Subaru, with new-type Impreza 555s (and Carlos Sainz!) were the major rivals.

However, and as that rallying sage Martin Holmes commented at the time: "Having a car which was inherently badly balanced compared with the cars of its rivals, which have longitudinally-mounted engines, this was the win it feared would never happen, but which did …"

Amazingly, Juha Kankkunen had recovered from his Safari smash, and preserved on this all-tarmac rally to take fourth place, but it was Didier Auriol who quite dominated from start to finish, taking 13 fastest times from 23 stages, and never ceding the lead to Sainz – though the gap at the end was just one minute: the third team member, Andrea Aghini, was third.

Quite suddenly, though, it seemed that World rallying had become more competitive than ever. On the Acropolis Rally which followed, Toyota were marched, dusty kilometre after dusty kilometre, by Subaru, Mitsubishi and Ford, and at the end of a gruelling, hot, 33-stage event, Kankkunen could only take third place, while Didier Auriol had to retire with a smashed sump after clouting a large rock on a typically-Acropolis stage: up to that moment he had been second.

Naturally, the team then sent two cars to Argentina, where Toyota had already won in 1991 and 1993. Although the stats show that Didier Auriol (*not* Juha Kankkunen) won yet another World event, it is easy to miss the fact that the winning margin (over Carlos Sainz's Subaru) was just six seconds. Didier was fastest on twelve of the twenty-nine stages, Sainz on fourteen of them, and the rally lead changed eleven times during the three days! Strangely, Juha Kankkunen was slightly off the pace, and had to retire, his Celica giving electrical trouble.

Once again, Toyota then entered a full team of three ST185s in the Rally of New Zealand (with Yoshio Fujimoto in the third car), for this event was close to Toyota's heart (and its geographical base!) – and the Celicas had won three times in the previous four seasons. Unhappily, Colin McRae was on absolutely tip-top form in his Subaru Impreza, setting many fastest times and making no mistakes. Juha Kankkunen gritted his teeth and settled for second place, while Didier Auriol recorded fifth, having suffered two small accidents along the way.

And still the pressure was on in Cologne. First of all, the team had to decide when to start using the new-type ST205 model (which was effectively Dieter Bulling's 'baby'), then it had to get cars ready for the 1000 Lakes Rally, and finally it had to decide whether to back Auriol or Kankkunen for the final push on the World Drivers' Championship. Honours were definitely equal in August, and either driver, no question, could still become Champion.

Before the 1000 Lakes, the ST205 was tested extensively, then pitted against 'works' Escort RS Cosworth opposition in the non-Championship Mantta 200 event, before the team decided to back Auriol, Kankkunen and various supported drivers in ST185s, while sending Tomas Jansson to contest the event in a Group N version of the new car.

In Finland, as it happened, there was good news, and bad news, for a fine second place finish by Didier Auriol secured Toyota's Makes' Championship crown for the second year, though outright victory went to Tommi Makinen's Ford Escort RS Cosworth, and the Group N ST205 ended its event off the road. Juha Kankkunen also rolled his ST185, so badly that a rear wheel and suspension was almost detached from the rest of the car. Re-starting, after 19 minutes lost for repairs, in 76th position, Juha then set thirteen fastest stage times on his way to climbing back to ninth place, but from this moment his personal World Championship ambitions were shot through.

The new-generation Group A ST205 finally made its debut in Australia, an event which did not qualify for World Championship points in 1994. Only one car, driven by Juha Kankkunen, made an appearance, and it finished a creditable second, only nine seconds behind Colin McRae's Subaru Impreza, but there were some problems with the engine's fuel supply system, and it was not quite as outstanding as hoped.

San Remo, which followed in October, confirmed that Auriol might yet win the Drivers' Championship – and it also showed that the new ST205 (as driven by Juha Kankkunen) was really no faster than the older ST185 (Auriol). The new car's handling seemed still to be suspect at first, so Kankkunen struggled to keep up with his French team-mate. In the end Auriol won the event by 21 seconds from Sainz, while Kankkunen ended up seventh, though he set more fastest stage times!

Because the Rally Catalunya was also a non-Championship qualifier in 1994, TTE ignored it, though privateer Enrico Bertone used an ex-works ST185 (which carried the identity of K-AM5362) to win the event on its behalf.

All now hung on the results of the British RAC Rally, which ran at the end of November. TTE entered three cars – a new ST205 for Kankkunen, and old-style ST185s for Auriol and Fujimoto. The battle – and battle it most assuredly was – was with a fleet of Ford Escort RS Cosworths, and a trio of Subaru Imprezas.

Although the archive shows that Colin McRae's Subaru took the honours, and that Kankkunen finished second in his ST205, it misses the fact that Sainz's Subaru was always a threat until the Spaniard crashed out of the event, and that Didier Auriol struggled to finish, let alone win the World Drivers' Championship.

After Sainz crashed out, Didier was assured of the Drivers' crown, but nearly failed to finish. First he lost four minutes on the first day, at Chatsworth after hitting a rock, then threw away ten minutes after rolling off the road, and lost a further four minutes when a turbo blew. In the end, it was a miracle that he could be thirty *minutes* off the pace, be running 94th at that stage, and still manage to finish sixth.

Team boss Ove Andersson was heard to explode at one point: "Do you think he even *wants* to be World Champion!"

But he was, and deservedly so. At the end of a momentous season, Toyota and Auriol had done all that could be required of them.

European Championship events

Compared with previous seasons, there was something of an upsurge in Toyota success at European Championship level. In a massive 53-event series seemingly dominated by Ford Escort RS Cosworths from various teams, Celica GT-Fours won 12 times, most of those victories being in cars which had been sold on to private teams by TTE. Francois Chatriot, in particular, was outstanding, with four outright wins – in the Boucles de Spa, Grasse Alpin, Alsace Vosges and Mont Blanc events.

Toyota's very first Group A ST205 was rallied in Australia in 1994, where Juha Kankkunen flung it around so successfully that he took second place to Colin McRae's Subaru, losing out by just nine seconds.

San Remo, Italy. Didier Auriol (right) and Bernard Occelli became World Rally Champions in 1994, when driving the highly-developed ST185 models.

In Europe, Juha Kankkunen drove the ST205 for the first time in the 1994 San Remo Rally. He struggled to keep up with Didier Auriol's ST185 and finished seventh.

1995

For all Toyota rally enthusiasts, 1995 will go down as one of the most eventful of all seasons for the Cologne-prepared cars. Right from the start of the season, it seemed, the new-type ST205 cars seemed to have difficulty in matching the record of the older-type Celicas, controversy seemed to lurk at every corner – and the brutal fact is the new car had to fight very hard against the Subaru Imprezas which seemed to improve steadily throughout the year. Interestingly enough, the old-type ST185 was still preferred to the ST205 on the Safari (though it had been out of production for some time).

Top drivers Didier Auriol and Juha Kankkunen were joined by Armin Schwarz (who had been with Mitsubishi in 1993 and 1994), George Donaldson took over from Phil Short as team manager (Phil had returned to the UK, and subsequently joined Ralliart/Mitsubishi). Castrol, of course, remained as the team's major sponsor.

The 1995-model GT-Four was a very high tech machine, as this detailed cockpit shot confirms. Drivers and co-drivers were all expected to know the electric function of every switch and module before they drove the car.

Bright lights, glitz, and glamour – all for Juha Kankkunen's ST205, which took third place in Monte Carlo in 1995. (Reproduced from the BP/Castrol Archive)

Although the scandal surrounding illegal turbochargers eventually meant that all the team's results for 1995 were annulled, for the record the author nevertheless still quotes the results actually achieved. The fact is that the ST205 was by no means as successful as the ST165 and ST185-types had been. It seemed that the development limits of this long-running platform and power train were reached – and there is evidence that Ing. Bulling was perhaps not as sympathetic to rally requirements as he had been, in an earlier life, to motor racing conditions.

Armin Schwarz struggling on in the gloom, close to Monte Carlo in 1995. Unhappily, his engine expired on this event. (Reproduced from the BP/Castrol Archive)

Armin Schwarz's brand-new ST205, in full flight on the 1995 Monte Carlo Rally. (Reproduced from the BP/Castrol Archive)

Didier Auriol rallied the ST205 for the first time in Monte Carlo in January 1995 – but, unhappily, crashed out of the event.

Since this was an ST205, on deep snow, using the narrowest possible studded tyres, this could only be the Swedish Rally. In 1995 Juha Kankkunen took fourth place.

The first signs of trouble came in Monte Carlo, where Juha Kankkunen could only set three fastest stage times (on his way to third place), and Auriol (who crashed his car) none at all. Things were even worse in Sweden, where Kankkunen once again defeated Auriol (but could only finish fourth), all the other official team cars being defeated by Thomas Radstrom in a Cologne-built ST205. Every team driver complained about the lack of power from the latest 34mm-restricted engines.

Things suddenly improved in Portugal, in March, where re-developed engines, with comprehensively altered electronic 'mapping' were fitted. Suddenly, Kankkunen seemed to be competitive again, and led the field for much of the event, though in the end had to settle for second place, just eight seconds – eight seconds only – behind Sainz's Subaru Impreza. Armin Schwarz was fourth and Didier Auriol fifth, though the Frenchman was lucky to survive a roll in his ST205.

The ST205 became Toyota's front line rally car in 1995, a season which was marred in controversy. On the Swedish Rally, Armin Schwarz took ninth place.

Although the ST205s were still competitive in 1995, they were no longer dominant in World Championship rallies. 1994 Champion, Didier Auriol, took fifth place in Portugal.

Juha Kankkunen spent most of the time on the absolute limit in Portugal 1995. In the end, his ST205 was fastest on thirteen stages but finished second overall – by just eight seconds. (Reproduced from the BP/Castrol Archive)

This, if only we had known it, may have been the first time that the ST205s used the illegal; turbocharger restrictor installations – for the leap in engine performance was certainly enough to indicate as much.

Because the East African Safari did not count for the World Championship in 1995, every leading team including Toyota sent neither A-team drivers, nor the latest cars to compete. Instead, they entrusted two old-type (ST185) cars to Yoshio Fujimoto and local-hero Ian Duncan instead, both of these being heavily rebuilt 1994 examples, for both the identities had been seen in that year. In an event where they had very little opposition, the Celicas always led. Although Duncan had to change a rear axle after his car hit rocks which seemed to have been placed in the road by vandals, he climbed back to third place, while Fujimoto himself won – in the end by a sturdy 42 minutes.

Although Japan often developed fine cars, it rarely produced World-class rally drivers. One honourable exception was Yoshio Fujimoto, who won the Safari Rally outright in 1995. He is seen here on the 1994 RAC Rally.

Back in Europe, three cars – for Auriol, Kankkunen and Schwarz – were entered in the Tour de Corse. Although all of them were outpaced by Bruno Thiry's Ford Escort RS Cosworth, that car hit trouble on a later stage, which left Didier Auriol to record his sixth outright victory on what was clearly his favourite all-tarmac rally: this was the first, in fact the only, World victory which the ill-fated ST205 would ever have. If only Juha Kankkunen had not gone off the road for five minutes, he might have finished higher than tenth place, but nevertheless, Toyota's spirits were high.

Because neither the Acropolis nor Argentina counted for World points, Toyota ignored both events, but was back in force for New Zealand (which was almost Toyota's 'home' event) instead. Although this event, somehow, seemed to suit the Subarus (Colin McRae in particular) better than anything else, the four cars sent from Cologne were all on the pace. At the end of what felt like a frighteningly fast event, Messrs Auriol/Kankkunen/Schwarz finished second/third/fourth, and set nineteen fastest stage times (out of a total of 30 stages). For Toyota, the way in which it had regained performance was almost too good to be true …

Perhaps it was just as well that the Finnish 1000 Lakes did not qualify for 'World' points in 1995, so no official team of cars made the trip. Juha Kankkunen started – this being because the 1000 Lakes was his 'home' event, but he retired after tearing off the front wheel on a protruding rock. Even so, privateer Marcus Gronholm, took second place overall.

Then came Rally Australia, where keen-eyed watchers saw just how much extra power the Toyotas now seemed to be developing, especially when they were seen submitting themselves to 'drag races' against the opposition at the Langley Park 'Superspecial' stage in Perth. For the whole of the first day, first Didier Auriol, then Juha Kankkunen led the entire event, and though Kenneth Eriksson's Mitsubishi Lancer Evo eventually won the event, and set most FTDs, the Celicas finished well up, in third, fifth and seventh places.

After a well used Grifone-entered car (K-AM806, driven by Andrea Dallavilla) took second place in the non-Championship San Remo event, the 'works' team then entered all its A-list drivers – Didier Auriol, Juha Kankkunen and Armin Schwarz – in the Catalunya Rally of Spain, which was centred on Lloret de Mar. Almost at once, among other teams and among FIA organisers and technical representatives, suspicion about the Celica's specifications arose – not merely because the cars looked so impressive, but because on this all-tarmac event it was Juha Kankunnen (who was known to dislike tarmac stages), who was demonstrably faster than the opposition.

Before the end of the first day, Jacques Berger of the FIA visited every 'works' team, demanded (and got) possession of all their spare turbochargers, and took them away for inspection. As one team manager later told the author: "The following day we got our turbos back, and didn't think any more about it, but we subsequently discovered that Toyota didn't get its back. By that time I believe that the FIA had become aware of the nature of the transgression …"

Until the bombshell exploded later in the event, the media seemed happy to credit Kankkunen with a total rejuvenation, but that soon changed. Well before half-distance Schwarz dropped out after an accident – *another* accident (TTE once calculated that he wrote off 14 shells in a complete season!), and on the second day Kankkunen mis-heard a pace note, left the road at high speed, and wrote off his car. Which left only Auriol still running, and those listening in on radio scanners heard that Toyota team management ordered him not to finish, rather than be disqualified (which he duly was …) after finishing.

What happened between TTE and the FIA scrutineers after the Catalunya Rally has already been analysed in the 'Car and the team' section. This is no criticism of the ST205 in general but, suffice to say, Toyota was instantly banned from the World Championship until the start of the 1997 season, and all team drivers had all their points removed from the Drivers' Championship in 1995. When this happened, both the team and Juha Kankkunen had been leading their respective series.

As a consequence, there were no 'works' Celicas in the last event of the year, the British RAC Rally, and the team's operations closed down in some disarray.

European Championships

As in World events, so in Europe, the Celicas (now in their eighth season of rallying) were finding it increasingly difficult to stay ahead of newer rivals. Even so, the records show that there were ten outright victories, that the Italian, Enrico Bertone won five times, and that he won the European Rally Championship outright. This, though, was the peak of the Celica's achievements in Europe.

1996

Although the official 'works' Toyota team was banned from rallying for the whole of 1996, there seemed to be nothing in that ruling to stop Cologne-prepared cars being loaned out, and entered by satellite teams, and driven by 'works' drivers. Gratifyingly, there would be further successes to make this subterfuge all worthwhile.

To quote Team Manager George Donaldson:

"We did a World Championship programme on events where importers wanted us to turn up, so we entered under the importers' names. For instance we did the Swedish, the Safari, Indonesia, Australia, Greece – we provided cars, drivers, teams, the whole thing. We still had sponsorship deals with Marlboro and Castrol – they wanted us to keep doing things, and they provided the money to do these programmes. We also ran a national Championship programme in Belgium."

As to drivers:

"Well, Didier had to be laid off, but Juha was kept on. Juha was really quite happy, especially as it gave him even more time to play lots of golf, and there was no Celica testing to be done …"

Because of the FIA's new – and much disliked – 'rotation' policy of not recognising every major event for the World series, the 1996 Monte Carlo Rally did not qualify, and was a low-key affair. Even so, two Cologne-registered cars started the Monte Carlo Rally (K-AM948 and K-AM6215), both of them having been seen in 'works' colours in the previous years. Armin Schwarz drove K-AM948 into a fine third place, though Gilberto Pianezzola's car crashed out on only the second stage.

Three cars from Cologne, 'on loan' to Toyota Castrol Team Sweden, started the Swedish Rally, that of Juha Kankkunen being a brand-new car (or, at least, carrying a brand-new identity). Although Juha set six fastest stage times in this snowy event, he could only finish fourth overall, even though he was only 88 seconds behind the winning car.

The Rally of Portugal was another event to suffer from the 'rotation' policy, which meant that no major 'works' teams took part. This, though, was an ideal chance for so-called 'private' Celicas (in this case from HF Grifone) to shine. On this occasion K-AM948 was driven to victory by local-hero Rui Madeira, and another new car (K-AM290 for Freddy Loix) took second place.

Three Cologne-registered cars – two of them actually being old-style ST185-types – took part in the Safari, where Ian Duncan's newly-built ST205 took third place, and others contested Indonesia (Kankkunen was third), but once Juha Kankkunen decided that he would rather drive for Ford (and M-Sport) in Escort RS Cosworths, the sting went out of the programme. Amazingly, Ford then released Juha to contest his 'home' event, the Neste/1000 Lakes Rally in August, where he took a brand-new ST205 to gain second place behind Tommi Makinen's Mitsubishi.

Significantly, the Celica's final victory came in the Network Q RAC Rally of 1996, another non-qualifying event because of the rotation policy, where Armin Schwarz used K-AM6361 to win outright, by an eight-minute margin.

1997

Proof that the Celica GT-Four's career was nearly all over came in 1997, but although Toyota Team Europe was almost entirely tied up with the development of the all-new Corolla World Rally Car (which made its World debut in the Neste 1000 Lakes in August), the hard-working team still had time to support loaned cars in several events, and to produce at least four brand-new identities for this final season.

Ian Duncan took third place on the Safari, Freddie Loix took second place in Portugal (only Tommi Makinen's Mitsubishi could beat him), Marcus Gronholm was fourth in Argentina, but this really was the end of a marvellous, decade-long, front line career.

GT-Fours were also winners at European Championship level. This was Freddie Loix's Marlboro-liveried car on its way to success in the Belgian Ypres Rally of 1996. The car was still maintained by Toyota in Cologne, though officially it was banned from entering 'official' cars throughout that year. (Reproduced from the BP/Castrol Archive)

Smile please – left to right: Lars Backman, Thomas Radstrom and Marcus Gronholm, ready to tackle the 1997 Swedish Rally as private entrants in ST205s. Radstrom took fifth place, and Gronholm eighth. (Reproduced from the BP/Castrol Archive)

What could succeed the Celica?

When Toyota was banned from World rallying at the end of 1995, the 'works' team immediately started working on a new rally car, its first (and, as it transpired, its only) World Rally Car. Whereas 5000 (a requirement later reduced to 2500) four-wheel-drive Celicas had needed to be built to achieve homologation, WRC regulations required only twenty identical cars (or kits of cars) to be made. This meant that Toyota (like rival teams) could use more extreme engineering solutions for its new car.

The new car, known as the Corolla World Rally Car, was designed in 1996, tested early in 1997, unveiled in July 1997, homologated on 1 August 1997, and was instantly competitive. The first podium finish came three months later, when Didier Auriol took third place in Australia, and the first outright victories would follow in 1998.

Although all the Celicas had been based on whichever Toyota sports coupe platform had been in production at the time, the Corolla WRC was to a completely new approach. For the very first time, Toyota chose to base its no-holds-barred World Rally Car design on the compact, three-door hatchback layout of the Corolla family car, which was normally an inoffensive little front-wheel-drive machine, sold in millions, and without performance pretensions.

Except that the same basic engine and transmission as the old Celicas – 1998cc turbocharged four-cylinder, and six-speed Xtrac gearbox – was used, almost every other detail of the car was new. In fact the transmission case was larger than before, for this would give space for a new and high tech 'active' system to be fitted at a later date.

Because both cars could get down to the minimum weight allowed by regulations, the unladen weight of both cars – 1230kg (2712lb) – was the same, though the new Corolla was inherently lighter, and could run with ballast screwed into the bodyshell to achieve the optimum weight distribution.

All in all, the new Corolla was more compact than before, with very little overhand. Both cars ran with a nominal 300bhp at 5600rpm. The new Corolla was an altogether more squat car than the last of the Celicas. In overall length, it was a massive 324mm (12.8in) shorter, and ran on a 57mm (2.25in) shorter wheelbase, but with a 54mm (2.1in) front track.

This was a good design which soon proved its point, and Toyota would certainly have made more of it if the top-level decision had not eventually been made to divert the motorsport department's attention to F1 in the early 2000s.

World/major European rally wins

Event	Car	Drivers
1988		
There was one victory in European Championship rallies		
1989		
Australia	K-AM5108	Kankkunen/Piironen
There were also 7 victories in European Championship rallies		
1990		
Safari	K-AM3910	Waldegård/Gallagher
Acropolis	K-AM3342	Sainz/Moya
New Zealand	PA7325	Sainz/Moya
1000 Lakes	K-AM8139	Sainz/Moya
RAC	K-AM7878	Sainz/Moya
There were also 6 victories in European Championship rallies		
1991		
Monte Carlo	K-AM1239	Sainz/Moya
Portugal	K-AM5914	Sainz/Moya
Corsica	K-AM422	Sainz/Moya
New Zealand	K-AM7878	Sainz/Moya
Argentina	K-AM1457	Sainz/Moya
Catalunya/Spain	K-AM2590	Schwarz/Hertz
There were also 2 victories in European Championship rallies		
1992		
Sweden	Private entry	Jonsson/Backman
Safari	K-AM3925	Sainz/Moya
New Zealand	K-AM6196	Sainz/Moya
Catalunya/Spain	K-AM2134	Sainz/Moya
RAC	K-AM2163	Sainz/Moya
There were also 6 victories in European Championship rallies		
1993		
Monte Carlo	K-AM5362	Auriol/Occelli
Sweden	K-AM7462	Johsson/Backman
Safari	K-AM51	Kankkunen/Piironen
Argentina	K-AM78	Kankkunen/Grist
1000 Lakes	K-AM828	Kankkunen/Giraudet
Australia	K-AM78	Kankkunen/Grist
RAC	K-AM828	Kankkunen/Grist
There were also 4 victories in European Championship events		
1994		
Sweden	-	Radstrom/Backman*
Portugal	K-AM9317	Kankkunen/Grist
Safari	K-AM4261	Duncan/Williamson
Corsica	K-AM9099	Auriol/Occelli
Argentina	K-AM8356	Auriol/Occelli
San Remo	K-AM6983	Auriol/Occelli
There were also 11 victories in European Championship events		
1995		
Safari	K-AM7737	Fujimoto/Hertz
Corsica	K-AM948	Auriol/Giraudet
There were also 12 victories in European Championship events		

*Private owner, supported by Toyota-Sweden

Works rally cars – World Championship rallies (and when first used)

Note: In the case of a German-registered car, one particular machine might carry more than one registration number during its life. This explains why so many different numbers appeared on 'works' GT-Fours in the period covered, for the number would be changed after a major rebuild (particularly after an accident had been rectified) was carried out. Even so, I have quoted numbers, if only to allow Celica followers to help identify cars from photographs!

Like all other serious 'works' rally teams of the 1980s and 1990s, if the monocoque of a Celica was too badly damaged to repair, a new car would be built up and prepared for motorsport, but using the old chassis plate, though with a different identity. In all cases, I have quoted the year in which a particular identity was first used.

1988
K-AM1988
K-AM2051
K-AM2924
K-AM2130
K-AM3787
K-AM4903
K-AM5265
K-AM5540
K-AM6782

1989
K-AM801
K-AM4135
K-AM5108 (Australia 1989)
K-AM6009
K-AM6108
K-AM6132
K-AM6223
K-AM6320
K-AM6330
K-AM7089

K-AM7516
K-AM8332
K-AM9444

1990
K-AM108
K-AM791
K-AM2623
K-AM3212
K-AM3342 (Acropolis 1990)
K-AM3564
K-AM3910 (Safari 1990)
K-AM4574
K-AM4575
K-AM5042
K-AM5803
K-AM7052
K-AM7878 (RAC 1990, New Zealand 1991)
K-AM8133
K-AM8139 (1000 Lakes 1990)
K-AM9801

PA7325 (NZ registration – New Zealand 1990 – was original K-AM8133)

1991
K-AM281
K-AM371
K-AM422 (Corsica 1991)
K-AM677
K-AM1239 (Monte Carlo 1991)
K-AM1457 (Argentina 1991)
K-AM1667
K-AM2480
K-AM2590 (Catalunya/Spain 1991)
K-AM2816
K-AM3767
K-AM4083
K-AM5914 (Portugal 1991)
K-AM6836
K-AM7070
K-AM8340
K-AM8798

K-AM8930

1992
The following were second-generation, ST185, 'Celica Turbo 4WD' types:

K-AM1014
K-AM1129
K-AM1694
K-AM2134 (Catalunya/Spain 1992)
K-AM2163 (RAC 1992)
K-AM2234
K-AM2504
K-AM3109
K-AM3390
K-AM3925 (Safari 1992)
K-AM6196 (New Zealand 1992)
K-AM6237
K-AM6836
K-AM7462
K-AM8202
K-AM8524
K-AM9223
K-AM9346
K-AM9821

1993
K-AM46
K-AM47
K-AM50
K-AM51 (Safari 1993)
K-AM52
K-AM54
K-AM72
K-AM78 (Argentina 1993, Australia 1993)
K-AM79
K-AM814
K-AM816
K-AM824
K-AM828 (1000 Lakes/Finland 1993, RAC 1993)
K-AM845
K-AM5362 (Monte Carlo 1993)
K-AM5951
K-AM7462 (Sweden 1993) GT4 (Swedish registration)

1994
K-AM703
K-AM1705
K-AM3405
K-AM4019
K-AM4177
K-AM4261 (Safari 1994)
K-AM5380
K-AM6162
K-AM6983 (San Remo 1994)
K-AM7737 (Safari 1995)
K-AM8356 (Argentina 1994)
K-AM9099 (Corsica 1994)
K-AM9317 (Portugal 1994)

Except where noted, the following were third-generation ST205 Celica GT4 types:

K-AM2339
K-AM5058
K-AM7098
K-AM8686

1995
K-AM806
K-AM864
K-AM926
K-AM948 (Corsica 1995)
K-AM1177
K-AM2188
K-AM2390
K-AM2555
K-AM2695
K-AM3103
K-AM3627
K-AM3648
K-AM4021
K-AM4993
K-AM5038
K-AM6215
K-AM7182
K-AM7291

1996
Following Toyota's retrospective disqualification from the 1995 World Championship, and from the 1996 series, too, no further official entries of Celica-based cars were made by TTE. The following, however, identifies newly-built or completely reconstructed cars from Cologne, which were 'loaned' out on occasion:

K-AM290
K-AM846
K-AM915
K-AM973
K-AM3003
K-AM5133
K-AM6361
K-AM7405

1997
K-AM828
K-AM3643
K-AM6366
K-AM8518

Index

Toyota references occur so frequently in the text that it is impractical to index separate models.

Abarth 35, 38
Andersson, Ove 9, 15-17, 21, 25, 29, 33, 38, 43-47, 53, 58, 64, 75, 89, 93, 102, 104
Andreasson, Solve 38
Audi (and models) 9-15, 20, 46
Autosport 84, 94

Bertl, Jurgen 38, 46
BMW (and models) 13, 18
Brundle, Martin 38
Bulling, Dieter 35-37, 40, 103, 107

Citroën (and models) 10, 49, 67

Datsun (and models) 10
DKW (and models) 10
Donaldson, George 37-39, 43, 46, 47, 49, 50, 67, 101, 106, 116

Endean, Mike 30

Fall, Tony 29
Fiat (and models) 10, 11, 91
Ford (and models) 11-15, 18, 19, 30, 35, 41, 43, 45-47, 49, 52, 55, 57, 58, 64, 72, 73, 75, 78, 80, 87, 89, 90, 93-96, 99-103, 115, 117
Frankfurt Motor Show 20

General Motors 15, 29

Goldstein, Karl-Heinz 29, 30
Guaslard, Maurice 34, 38, 46, 67

Hainbach, Reinhard 46
Holmes, Martin 33, 83, 102

Issigonis, Sir Alec 10

Jolly Club 74, 87, 90, 96

Klein, Reinhard 29

Lancia (and models) 12-15, 17-20, 30, 32, 33, 35, 38, 39, 43, 47, 49, 50, 52, 55, 59, 62, 64, 65, 67, 68, 72-75, 78-81, 83-85, 87, 89-92, 95, 96, 101
Liddon, Henry 38, 43, 45, 46

Mazda (and models) 13, 18, 31, 65, 72
Meade, Bill 45
Mini (and models) 10
Mitsubishi (and models) 13, 18, 35, 41, 46, 62, 63, 65, 72-74, 81, 84, 94-96, 100, 102, 106, 115, 117
Mosley, Max 41, 42
M-Sport 46, 117

Opel (and models) 29, 31
Oswin, Keith 94

Peugeot (and models) 14, 15, 43, 49
Pfeiffer, Gerhard 29, 38
Prodrive 18, 38

Ralliart 46, 106
Rallies:
　Acropolis 11, 14, 31, 38, 39, 53, 54, 59, 67, 70, 75, 78, 81, 84, 90, 91, 96, 102, 115, 117
　Alsace Vosges 104
　Argentina 68, 71, 72, 81, 83, 84, 90, 91, 96, 97, 101, 102, 115, 117
　Australia 35, 36, 39-41, 58, 62, 73, 85, 91, 98-100, 103, 104, 115, 117, 118
　Boucles de Spa 64, 104
　Cartel 76
　Circuit of Ireland 63, 75
　Cyprus 55
　Grasse Alpin 104
　Hunsruck 55
　Indonesia 117
　Ivory Coast (also called Bandama) 11, 13, 45, 46, 73, 92
　Mantta 200 103
　Mont Blanc 104
　Monte Carlo 11, 32, 43, 52, 59, 60, 65, 66, 78, 87, 94, 100, 107-111, 117

New Zealand 58, 67, 71, 81-84, 90, 91, 96, 98, 103, 115
Portugal 33, 52, 59, 65, 78, 89, 101, 111-113, 117
RAC of Great Britain 10, 47, 52, 55-57, 62, 64, 73-75, 82, 85, 92, 93, 99, 100, 103, 114, 115, 117
Safari 11, 13, 25, 35, 43, 47, 59, 67-69, 78, 79, 89, 94-96, 101, 102, 106, 114, 117
San Remo 55, 62, 73, 74, 85, 92, 99, 103, 105, 115
South Sweden 64, 93
Spain (Catalunya) 35, 40-42, 84, 85, 92, 93, 99, 103, 115
Swedish 52, 65, 87, 88, 94, 101, 110, 111, 117, 118
1000 Lakes (Finland) 31, 36, 52, 55, 59, 72, 73, 91, 92, 96, 99, 100, 103, 115, 117
Tour de Corse (Corsica) 18, 19, 30, 31, 33, 35, 37, 50, 52-54, 59, 61, 67, 70, 79, 84, 89, 95, 102, 115
Ulster 75, 76
World Cup Rally (1974) 45
Ypres 117
Rally drivers from rival teams:
  Alen, Markku 55, 74
  Andersson, Ove 45
  Airikkala, Pentti 18, 63, 74
  Auriol, Didier 35, 50, 52, 59, 65, 67, 68, 73, 74, 78, 80, 81, 91, 92
  Biasion, Miki 59, 68, 78, 87, 89
  Delecour, Francois 35, 78, 80, 89, 94, 96, 99, 101, 102
  Ericcson, Mikael 18
  Eriksson, Kenneth 74, 81, 100, 115
  Fiorio, Alex 91
  Harris, Nigel 45
  Kahlfuss, Michael 102
  Kankkunen, Juha 65, 67, 72-74, 81, 84, 85, 89, 92, 117
  Makinen, Timo 45
  Makinen, Tommi 18, 103, 117
  McRae, Colin 93, 96, 100, 103, 115
  Mikkola, Hannu 18, 74
  Sainz, Carlos 57, 93, 99, 102, 103, 111
  Salonen, Timo 18, 35, 74
  Thiry, Bruno 115
  Vatanen, Ari 18, 72, 74, 92, 98
  Wilson, Malcolm 93
Range Rover 15
Renault (and models) 10, 43
Rohrer, Dagobert 38

Saab (and models) 10
Senna, Ayrton 102
Short, Phil 38, 39, 43, 46, 47, 50, 93, 102, 106
Subaru (and models) 15, 35, 38, 41, 47, 50, 92, 93, 96, 98, 100, 102, 103, 106, 115

Toyota rally drivers:
  Aghini, Andrea 100-102
  Alen, Markku 34, 72, 86, 88-95
  Asterhag, Lief 87, 88
  Auriol, Didier 35, 50, 93, 94, 96-103, 105, 106, 110-112, 115, 117, 118
  Backman, Lars 118
  Bertone, Enrico 103
  Bin Sulayem, Mohammed 77, 83, 86
  Chatriot, Francois 104
  Dallavilla, Andrea 115
  Diekmann, Peter 44, 52
  Duez, Marc 100, 102
  Duncan, Ian 59, 94, 95, 101, 102, 114, 117
  Ericsson, Mikael 66, 67, 72, 74, 78, 83, 89
  Eriksson, Kenneth 44, 52-55, 58, 59, 62, 63
  Fujimoto, Yoshio 102, 103, 114
  Gallagher, Fred 57
  Giraudet, Denis 96
  Grist, Nicky 96, 99, 100, 102

123

Gronholm, Marcus 91, 115, 117, 118
Hertz, Arne 29
Iwase, Yasuhiro 94, 95
Jansson, Tomas 103
Jonsson, Mats 84, 87, 94, 100
Kankkunen, Juha 30, 35, 42, 44, 49, 50, 52-55, 58-65, 93-107, 110, 111, 113, 115, 117
Llewellin, David 46, 55, 57, 63, 64, 74-76, 85
Loix, Freddy 117
Mikkola, Hannu 96, 98
Morgan, Ronan 77, 86
Moya, Luis 67, 70, 71, 75, 85
Occelli, Bernard 105
Pianezzola, Gilberto 117
Piironen, Juha 44, 54, 96
Radstrom, Thomas 101, 111, 118
Sainz, Carlos 8, 23, 25, 34, 35, 47-50, 57-59, 63-68, 70-75, 78-87, 89-93
Schwarz, Armin 65, 74, 78-80, 84-87, 89-92, 93, 106, 108, 109, 111, 115
Snyers, Patrick 46, 59, 64
Waldegård, Björn 14, 30, 44, 52, 53, 55-59, 67, 68, 78
Wittman, Franz 100
Trabant 601R 102

VW (and models) 10

World Rallying 14, 83

RALLY GIANTS

ISBN: 978-1-787113-24-4

ISBN: 978-1-787111-08-0

ISBN: 978-1-787111-11-0

ISBN: 978-1-787113-25-1

ISBN: 978-1-787113-22-0

ISBN: 978-1-787111-10-3

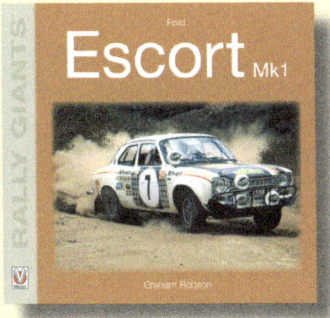
ISBN: 978-1-787111-07-3

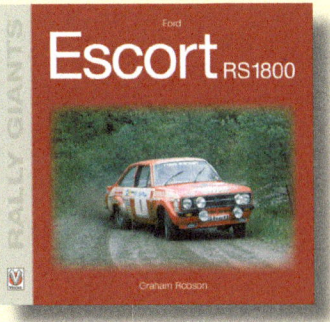
ISBN: 978-1-787111-09-7

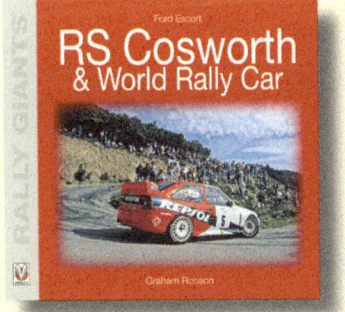
ISBN: 978-1-787111-71-4

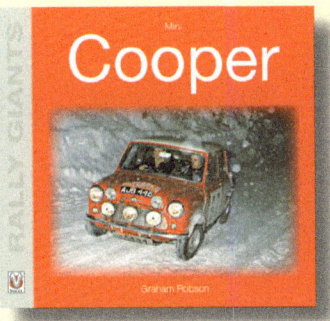
ISBN: 978-1-84584-183-6

ISBN: 978-1-787113-31-2

ISBN: 978-1-845842-58-1

Lancia 037 – The development & rally history of a World Champion
Hardback • 25x25cm
• 224 pages • 300 mainly colour photos
• ISBN: 978-1-787111-28-8

The story of Lancia's mid-engined and supercharged 037, the car that dominated Group B rallying in the eighties. Featuring many of Chief Designer Sergio Limone's own photographs taken during development, as well as interviews with team members, this is the definitive history of a true world champion.

BMC Competitions Department Secrets
Paperback • 25x20.7cm
• 192 pages • 217 pictures
• ISBN: 978-1-845849-94-8

Reprinted after a long absence! For the London to Sydney Marathon, team instructions included the recommendation that a firearm be carried by the crew of each car ... "A small pistol which can conveniently be located under cover in the car is what we have in mind" ...

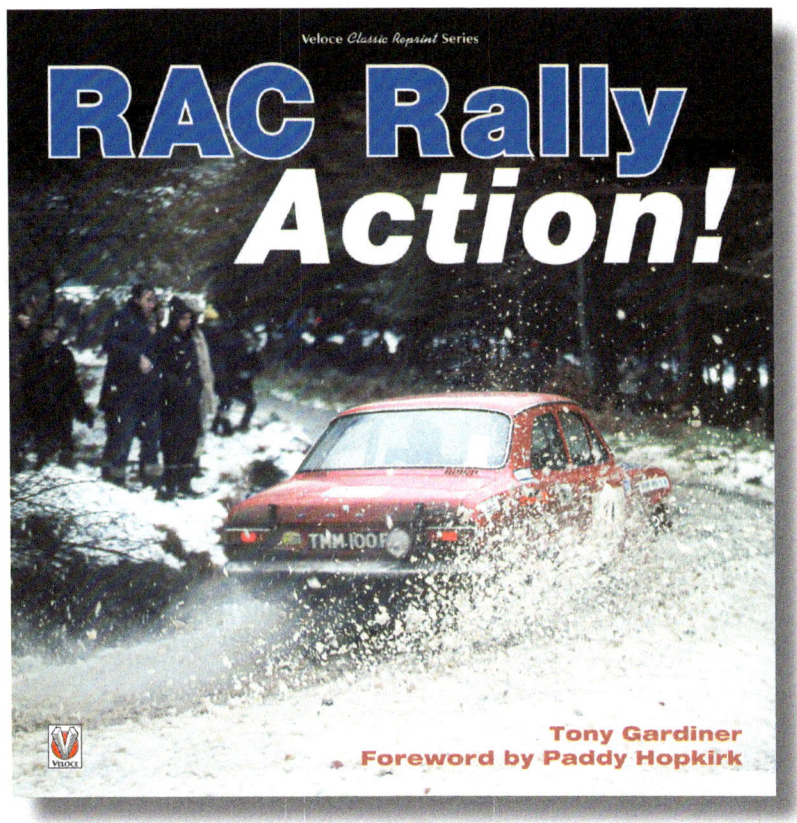

RAC Rally Action!
Hardback • 25x25cm
• 208 pages • 330 colour & b&w photos
• ISBN: 978-1-787112-29-2

This book covers the pre-WRC golden years, the Rally of the Forests period. With access to crew notes and manufacturers' archives, and containing many previously unpublished pictures, the history and excitement of the RAC International Rally of Great Britain has been captured forever in Tony Gardiner's book.

For more information on these and other great Veloce books:
visit www.veloce.co.uk • email info@veloce.co.uk • or call +44 (0)1305 260068

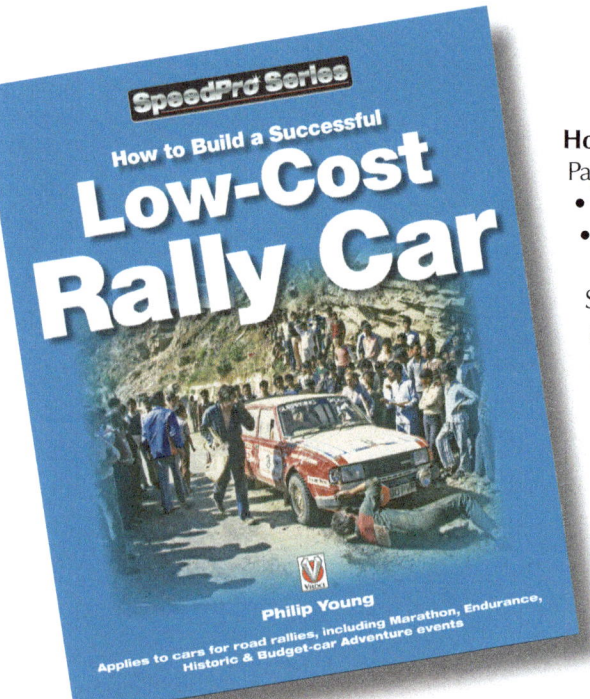

How to Build a Successful Low-Cost Rally Car
Paperback • 25x20.7cm
- 96 pages • 150 colour pictures
- ISBN: 978-1-845842-08-6

Simple, cost-effective, basic and reliable tips to ensure any rally car stands a chance of reaching the finishing line. If you are planning a road-based rally, don't even think of leaving home before reading this book, and implementing the tried and tested mods it describes so well.

Works rally mechanic
Paperback • 25x20.7cm
- 160 pages • 159 colour & b&w photos
- ISBN: 978-1-787113-30-5

For 22 years Brian prepared cars for international rallies, providing service support for 'Big' Healeys, Minis and TR7s. Adventure, hilarious events, hardship, winning, losing, & real danger …

"The stories that this 22-year veteran of the Abingdon-based British Motor Corporation/British Leyland Competitions Department shares chronicle the evolution of the 'works,' and the corporate policies that shaped its existence … fans of BMC/British Leyland cars will also enjoy a treasure of rarely seen photographs, many of which came from the personal collections of the author and his co-workers; 'Works Rally Mechanic' is a must for any Anglophile's bookshelf." – Hemmings Sports & Exotic Car

Printed and bound by CPI Group (UK) Ltd, Croydon, CR0 4YY
22/03/2026
02076064-0008